I0427526

STOIC ENTREPRENEUR

Embracing Ancient Wisdom for
Modern Success in Business

*Featuring practical exercises and
prompts for business growth*

Ceballos Alanis

1

Copyright @ 2024 by Ceballos Alanis

All rights reserved. No part of this publication may be reproduced, distributed or transmitted in any form or by any means, including photocopying, recording, or other electronic or mechanical methods, without the prior written permission of the publisher, except in the case of brief quotations embodied in critical reviews and certain other noncommercial uses permitted by copyright law.

ACKNOWLEDGMENTS

Gratitude to Stoic Philosophers

Expressing gratitude to Stoic philosophers is a profound acknowledgment of the timeless wisdom they have bequeathed to humanity, particularly in the realm of Stoic entrepreneurship. Their teachings, rooted in ancient philosophy, continue to guide individuals on a transformative journey of self-discovery, resilience, and ethical leadership. Here, we express gratitude to the key Stoic philosophers who have shaped the principles that resonate in the entrepreneurial landscape:

ZENO OF CITIUM: The founder of Stoicism, Zeno, laid the philosophical foundation that has endured over two millennia. His teachings on living in accordance with nature and understanding the dichotomy of control serve as fundamental pillars for entrepreneurs navigating the uncertainties of business. Gratitude is extended to Zeno for providing the philosophical framework that empowers individuals to focus on what lies within their control and accept the rest with equanimity.

EPICTETUS: Born into slavery, Epictetus emerged as a prominent Stoic philosopher whose teachings on resilience, personal agency, and ethical conduct resonate deeply with entrepreneurs. Gratitude is extended to Epictetus for his practical insights on distinguishing between what is in our power and what is not, fostering a mindset that is foundational for navigating the challenges of entrepreneurship.

SENECA: A statesman, philosopher, and playwright, Seneca's contributions to Stoicism include profound reflections on virtue, adversity, and ethical decision-making. Entrepreneurs express gratitude to Seneca for his wisdom on cultivating inner resilience, embracing challenges as opportunities, and navigating the complexities of wealth and success with virtue.

MARCUS AURELIUS: As a Roman Emperor and Stoic philosopher, Marcus Aurelius' "Meditations" stand as a timeless guide for ethical leadership and self-reflection. Entrepreneurs express profound gratitude to Marcus Aurelius for his insights on humility, duty, and the pursuit of virtue, providing a moral compass for those in positions of leadership.

THE STOIC COMMUNITY: Gratitude extends to the broader Stoic community, including modern scholars, practitioners, and enthusiasts who have contributed to the revival and dissemination of Stoic principles. Through books, lectures, podcasts, and online forums, this community has played a vital role in making Stoicism accessible to contemporary audiences, including entrepreneurs seeking guidance in their professional journeys.

In expressing gratitude to Stoic philosophers, entrepreneurs recognize the enduring impact of their teachings. The Stoic legacy continues to inspire individuals to cultivate resilience, lead with virtue, and navigate the dynamic landscape of entrepreneurship with wisdom and purpose. The debt of gratitude extends not only to the historical figures who shaped Stoicism but also to the collective efforts of those who ensure that Stoic wisdom remains a beacon for ethical and resilient business practices in the modern world.

Thanks to Influential Entrepreneurs

Expressing gratitude to influential entrepreneurs is a recognition of the indelible mark they have left on the landscape of business, inspiring and shaping the entrepreneurial journey for others. These visionaries, through their innovations, leadership, and commitment to principles, have not only built successful enterprises but have also contributed to the broader understanding of ethical, purpose-driven business practices. Here, we extend thanks to some influential entrepreneurs who have made a significant impact:

ELON MUSK: Gratitude is extended to Elon Musk for his audacity in challenging the status quo across multiple industries, from electric vehicles with Tesla to space exploration with SpaceX. Musk's relentless pursuit of innovation and commitment to sustainable technologies serves as an inspiration for entrepreneurs aspiring to make a positive impact on the world.

OPRAH WINFREY: As a media mogul, philanthropist, and inspirational figure, Oprah Winfrey has transformed the media landscape and paved the way for a new era of personal development and empowerment. Entrepreneurs express thanks to Oprah for her leadership in demonstrating the power of storytelling, authenticity, and the profound impact of purpose-driven business ventures.

WARREN BUFFETT: Gratitude is extended to Warren Buffett for his exceptional acumen in the world of finance and investments. As one of the most successful investors of our time, Buffett's emphasis on long-term value, ethical decision-making, and simplicity in business practices provides valuable lessons for entrepreneurs navigating the complexities of financial stewardship.

STEVE JOBS: The late Steve Jobs, co-founder of Apple Inc., revolutionized the technology industry and redefined the consumer experience. Entrepreneurs express thanks to Jobs for his commitment to design excellence, innovation, and the relentless pursuit of perfection, setting a standard for visionary leadership.

INDRA NOOYI: Gratitude is extended to Indra Nooyi for her trailblazing leadership as the former CEO of PepsiCo. Nooyi's emphasis on purpose-driven business, sustainability, and diversity has left an enduring impact on corporate leadership. Entrepreneurs appreciate her dedication to social responsibility and inclusive leadership.

RICHARD BRANSON: As the founder of the Virgin Group, Richard Branson has been a pioneer in various industries, from music to space travel. Entrepreneurs express thanks to Branson for his adventurous spirit, emphasis on employee well-being, and commitment to using business as a force for positive change.

JACK MA: Gratitude is extended to Jack Ma for co-founding Alibaba Group, transforming e-commerce in China and globally. Entrepreneurs appreciate Ma's emphasis on resilience, adaptability, and his vision for enabling small businesses to thrive in the digital age.

ANITA RODDICK: The late Anita Roddick, founder of The Body Shop, is remembered for her commitment to ethical business practices, sustainability, and activism. Entrepreneurs express thanks to Roddick for paving the way for socially conscious enterprises and highlighting the importance of business with a conscience.

In expressing gratitude to these influential entrepreneurs, individuals acknowledge the role models and trailblazers who have shaped the entrepreneurial landscape. Their contributions extend beyond financial success to encompass ethical leadership, innovation, and a commitment to making a positive impact on the world. Through their collective influence, these entrepreneurs have inspired a new generation of business leaders to strive for excellence, purpose, and the betterment of society.

Success in business requires not only industry and capability but also the wisdom to discern between what is truly necessary and what is merely desirable. A shrewd entrepreneur recognizes that wealth is a means, not an end, and that true prosperity lies in the harmony of ethical conduct and prudent decision-making. In the pursuit of enterprise, one must remain undeterred by external circumstances, for the stoic entrepreneur understands that challenges are not impediments but opportunities for growth. The key to lasting success lies not in the accumulation of wealth alone but in the cultivation of virtue and the pursuit of a purpose higher than mere profit.... Lucius Annaeus Seneca

SYNOPSIS

In the fast-paced world of business, the Stoic Entrepreneur emerges as a guiding light, blending timeless principles from Stoic philosophy with modern entrepreneurial wisdom. This transformative book explores the profound intersection between Stoicism and business, revealing how ancient insights can illuminate the path to enduring success and fulfillment. Delving into the teachings of Stoic luminaries like Seneca, Marcus Aurelius, and Epictetus, the author intricately weaves their timeless wisdom into the fabric of contemporary entrepreneurship. Readers embark on a journey that transcends conventional success metrics, urging them to cultivate virtues like resilience, adaptability, and ethical leadership. The Stoic Entrepreneur confronts challenges as opportunities, acknowledging that external circumstances are beyond one's control, while internal virtues remain the compass for decision-making. The book navigates through the Stoic principles of wisdom, courage, justice, and temperance, illustrating how they become powerful tools for navigating the complexities of the business landscape.

Through real-world examples, practical insights, and thought-provoking exercises, the Stoic Entrepreneur offers a blueprint for building a business grounded in purpose, resilience, and ethical conduct. This book is not merely a guide to financial success but a transformative manual for those seeking a deeper, more meaningful entrepreneurial journey. Join the ranks of Stoic Entrepreneurs and discover how embracing ancient wisdom can redefine success, enrich personal fulfillment, and leave a lasting legacy in the dynamic world of business.

TABLE OF CONTENTS

INTRODUCTION

Purpose of the book

The purpose of "Stoic Entrepreneur": Daily Meditations for Resilient Leadership" is to provide a practical and insightful guide for entrepreneurs seeking to integrate Stoic philosophy into their daily lives and business practices. In the fast-paced and often unpredictable world of entrepreneurship, the Stoic principles offer timeless wisdom that can foster resilience, clarity, and ethical decision-making. This book aims to bridge the gap between ancient Stoic teachings and the modern challenges faced by entrepreneurs. It recognizes that the entrepreneurial journey is fraught with uncertainties, setbacks, and demanding decision points. By presenting daily meditations rooted in Stoic philosophy, the book equips entrepreneurs with the tools to navigate these challenges with a stoic mindset. Each section of the book corresponds to a month, offering a thematic structure that aligns with the cyclical nature of Stoic reflections. Readers will find daily doses of inspiration, practical advice, and thought-provoking exercises designed to cultivate Stoic virtues such as wisdom, courage, justice, and temperance. The meditations explore topics ranging from vision and resilience to leadership, time management, and ethical considerations.

The purpose extends beyond the individual development of entrepreneurs; it encompasses the creation of a Stoic-informed business culture. By encouraging leaders to apply Stoic principles in their decision-making, communication, and team management, the book envisions a ripple effect that positively influences the broader entrepreneurial ecosystem. *Ultimately, this book aspires to be a trusted companion on the entrepreneurial journey, offering daily insights that inspire self-reflection and growth. It emphasizes the integration of Stoic philosophy not as a theoretical concept, but as a practical guide for building a resilient and purpose-driven business.* As readers engage with the daily meditations, they will be empowered to face challenges with greater clarity, lead with virtue, and leave a lasting impact on both their businesses and the world.

Why Stoicism for Entrepreneurs?

Stoicism serves as a profound and practical philosophy for entrepreneurs navigating the dynamic and unpredictable landscape of business. Rooted in ancient Greek philosophy, Stoicism is characterized by its emphasis on virtue, wisdom, and resilience in the face of adversity. Here are several compelling reasons why Stoicism is particularly relevant and beneficial for entrepreneurs:

- **Resilience in the Face of Challenges:** Entrepreneurship is inherently challenging, with setbacks and failures being inevitable. Stoicism teaches individuals to view challenges as opportunities for growth, emphasizing the importance of maintaining composure in the face of adversity. Entrepreneurs can draw on Stoic principles to build emotional resilience and navigate uncertainties with a steady and focused mindset.

- **Clarity of Purpose:** Stoicism encourages individuals to reflect on their values and priorities, fostering a deep sense of purpose. For entrepreneurs, who often face competing demands and high-stakes decisions, having a clear sense of purpose can guide ethical decision-making and provide a solid foundation for long-term success.

- **Effective Decision-Making:** Stoicism emphasizes rationality and objective thinking. Entrepreneurs can benefit from this by making decisions based on sound judgment rather than being swayed by emotions or external pressures. Stoicism encourages a methodical approach to problem-solving, leading to more effective and thoughtful decision-making.

- **Adaptability and Flexibility:** The Stoic philosophy encourages individuals to focus on what they can control and accept what they cannot. In the dynamic world of entrepreneurship, unexpected changes are inevitable. Stoicism equips entrepreneurs with the mindset to adapt to changing circumstances, fostering a flexible and agile approach to business challenges.

- **Balanced Ambition:** While ambition is a driving force for entrepreneurs, Stoicism guides individuals to pursue success with temperance and humility. This balanced approach helps entrepreneurs avoid the pitfalls of excessive ambition, promoting sustainable and ethical business practices.

By integrating Stoic principles into their mindset and decision-making processes, entrepreneurs can not only navigate the complexities of business more effectively but also cultivate a sense of purpose and resilience that extends beyond their professional endeavors, enriching their personal lives as well.

How to Use This Book

Stoic Entrepreneur: Daily Meditations for Resilient Leadership" is designed to be a practical and transformative guide for entrepreneurs, providing a structured approach to integrating Stoic philosophy into their daily lives and business practices. To effectively harness the wisdom within this book, readers are encouraged to follow a purposeful and intentional approach.

- **Daily Engagement:** The book is organized into daily meditations, with each month focusing on a specific theme related to Stoic principles. Readers are encouraged to engage with one meditation per day, allowing time for reflection and practical application. This daily commitment helps build a consistent and ingrained Stoic mindset over the course of the year.

- **Thematic Monthly Structure:** Each month addresses different aspects of Stoic philosophy relevant to entrepreneurship. Readers can explore themes such as visions, resilience, leadership, ethics, and mindfulness. The thematic structure provides a coherent and progressive journey, allowing entrepreneurs to delve deeper into specific areas of personal and professional development.

- **Reflective Exercises:** Throughout the book, readers will find practical exercises and prompts accompanying each meditation. These exercises are designed to encourage introspection, application of Stoic principles to real-world scenarios, and the cultivation of practical skills. Entrepreneurs are encouraged to engage actively with these exercises to enhance their understanding and application of Stoic philosophy.

- **Personalization:** Stoicism is not a one-size-fits-all philosophy, and its application can vary from person to person. Readers are encouraged to personalize their experience by adapting the daily meditations and exercises to their unique entrepreneurial journey. This personalization fosters a deeper connection with Stoic principles and allows for more meaningful integration into daily practices.

- **Continuous Reflection:** The book includes a conclusion that encourages readers to reflect on key lessons learned throughout the year. This prompts entrepreneurs to revisit and reinforce their understanding of Stoic principles, ensuring that the benefits extend beyond the initial reading period.

By actively engaging with the daily meditations, incorporating reflective exercises, and adapting the content to their individual experiences, readers can use "Stoic Entrepreneur" as a transformative tool for developing resilience, ethical leadership, and a purpose-driven approach to entrepreneurship.

FOUNDATIONS OF STOICISM

Brief Overview of Stoicism

Stoicism, a philosophical school of thought that originated in ancient Greece, provides a timeless framework for individuals seeking wisdom, resilience, and virtue in the face of life's challenges. Dating back to early philosophers such as Zeno of Citium in the 3rd century BCE, Stoicism became a guiding principle for many including Epictetus, Seneca, and Marcus Aurelius, leaving a profound impact on Western philosophy. At its core, Stoicism revolves around the pursuit of eudaimonia, a state of flourishing achieved through the cultivation of virtues and alignment with nature. The philosophy emphasizes the importance of personal virtue, rationality, and self-discipline as means to attain tranquility and inner peace, irrespective of external circumstances.

Stoicism consists of several key principles that form the foundation of its teachings:

- **Nature and Reason:** Stoicism posits that individuals should live in harmony with the natural order of the universe. Reason is viewed as the highest faculty, guiding individuals to make sound judgments and act in accordance with virtue.
- **Virtue as the Highest Good:** The Stoics identified four cardinal virtues—wisdom, courage, justice, and temperance. These virtues are considered the path to a virtuous and fulfilled life, with the pursuit of virtue being prioritized over external goods and pleasures.

- **Acceptance of the External:** Stoicism teaches the distinction between what is within one's control and what is not. While individuals have control over their thoughts, actions, and choices, external events are often beyond their influence. Stoics advocate for acceptance of external outcomes, focusing instead on internal attitudes and responses.
- **Endurance and Resilience:** The philosophy places a strong emphasis on enduring hardship with equanimity. Stoics believe that challenges and adversity are inevitable aspects of life, and one's response to them determines their character and well-being.

In the context of entrepreneurship, Stoicism provides entrepreneurs with a practical and applicable set of principles for navigating the uncertainties and challenges of business. By embracing Stoic virtues and applying its teachings, individuals can foster resilience, ethical decision-making, and a sense of purpose in both their personal and professional lives. The "Brief Overview of Stoicism" in this book serves as a foundation for entrepreneurs to integrate these profound teachings into their daily practices and leadership approaches.

Stoic Principles for Entrepreneurs

Stoicism, an ancient philosophy that has withstood the test of time, offers a set of principles uniquely suited to guide entrepreneurs through the challenges and uncertainties of the business world. Rooted in virtues such as wisdom, courage, justice, and temperance, Stoicism provides a practical framework for ethical decision-making, resilience in the face of adversity, and the cultivation of a purpose-driven mindset.

1. Virtue as the Highest Good: The Stoic concept of virtue serves as the cornerstone for entrepreneurs seeking enduring success. Wisdom, courage, justice, and temperance are not merely ideals; they are actionable virtues that shape ethical conduct in business. Entrepreneurs embracing these virtues prioritize moral excellence, fostering a workplace culture rooted in integrity and principled leadership.

2. Dichotomy of Control: The dichotomy of control, a fundamental Stoic principle, distinguishes between what is within one's control and what is not. Entrepreneurs face a myriad of external factors—market trends, economic shifts, and competition—that are beyond their control. Stoicism encourages entrepreneurs to focus on internal aspects, such as decision-making and mindset, allowing them to navigate uncertainties with resilience and maintain equanimity in the face of uncontrollable external events.

3. Acceptance of the Present Moment: Entrepreneurs often find themselves immersed in future-oriented pursuits, striving for success and growth. Stoicism urges individuals to embrace the present moment, acknowledging both triumphs and challenges without excessive attachment or aversion. This principle fosters a mindful entrepreneurial mindset, helping leaders make decisions grounded in the reality of the current circumstances.

4. Practical Wisdom: Practical wisdom, a key Stoic virtue, emphasizes rational decision-making based on objective and informed judgment. Entrepreneurs can apply this principle by cultivating a deep understanding of their industry, market dynamics, and ethical considerations. Practical wisdom guides entrepreneurs to make sound, well-informed decisions that align with their values and long-term objectives.

5. Endurance and Resilience: The path of an entrepreneur is fraught with difficulties, disappointments, and uncertainty. Stoicism's emphasis on endurance encourages entrepreneurs to view obstacles as opportunities for growth rather than insurmountable barriers. By cultivating resilience, entrepreneurs not only weather the storms of business but also emerge stronger, more capable leaders.

6. Mindful Action and Intention: Mindfulness, a principle integral to Stoicism, encourages entrepreneurs to be fully present in their actions and decisions. By approaching tasks with intention and focus, entrepreneurs avoid impulsive reactions and navigate challenges with a clear and purposeful mindset. Mindfulness becomes a tool for effective decision-making and strategic planning.

7. Community and Social Responsibility: Stoicism underscores the interconnectedness of humanity, emphasizing the importance of justice and social responsibility. Entrepreneurs are urged to consider the broader impact of their actions on society. This principle guides ethical business practices, responsible corporate citizenship, and a consideration of the well-being of all stakeholders, contributing to the greater good.

In the dynamic and often unpredictable world of entrepreneurship, Stoicism serves as a beacon of wisdom and resilience. By incorporating these Stoic principles into their daily practices, entrepreneurs can foster a resilient and purpose-driven approach to business. Stoicism not only provides a philosophical foundation but also equips entrepreneurs with actionable tools for ethical leadership, effective decision-making, and sustained success. As entrepreneurs embrace these principles, they embark on a transformative journey, cultivating virtues that not only elevate their professional endeavors but also enrich their lives with meaning and purpose.

Applying Stoic Wisdom in Business

Stoic philosophy, with its emphasis on virtue, rationality, and resilience, provides a valuable framework for entrepreneurs seeking to navigate the complex terrain of business with ethical integrity and purpose. Applying Stoic wisdom in business goes beyond theoretical concepts; it offers actionable principles that can shape decision-making, leadership, and organizational culture.

1. Ethical Decision-Making: At the heart of Stoicism lies a commitment to virtue, and for entrepreneurs, this translates into ethical decision-making. By prioritizing wisdom, courage, justice, and temperance, business leaders can ensure that their choices align with moral principles. Stoicism encourages entrepreneurs to weigh decisions not just in terms of profitability but also in terms of their impact on employees, customers, and the broader community.

2. Resilience in the Face of Adversity: Stoicism teaches that challenges are an inherent part of life, and business is no exception. Entrepreneurs can apply Stoic principles to develop resilience in the face of setbacks. Instead of succumbing to despair or frustration, leaders can view obstacles as opportunities for growth. This resilience enables entrepreneurs to adapt to changing circumstances and persevere through the inevitable ups and downs of the business landscape.

3. Focus on the Controllable: Stoicism's dichotomy of control encourages entrepreneurs to differentiate between what is within their control and what is not. Business leaders often grapple with external factors such as market trends or economic shifts. By focusing on internal aspects—strategy, decision-making processes, and company culture—entrepreneurs can maintain a sense of control over their own actions and responses.

4. Mindful Leadership: Mindfulness, a key aspect of Stoic practice, encourages leaders to be present in their decision-making and interactions. Mindful leadership involves deliberate attention to the current moment, fostering clarity and preventing impulsive reactions. Entrepreneurs who adopt this approach can make decisions based on rational analysis rather than emotional turbulence.

5. Balanced Ambition: Stoicism encourages entrepreneurs to pursue success with temperance and humility. While ambition is a driving force in business, excessive desire for wealth or power can lead to ethical compromises. Stoic wisdom guides leaders to set ambitious goals while maintaining a balance that aligns with virtuous principles.

6. Team Collaboration and Justice: Stoicism emphasizes the interconnectedness of humanity, underscoring the importance of justice. In a business context, this translates into fair treatment of employees, customers, and partners. By fostering a sense of justice within the organization, leaders contribute to a positive and ethical workplace culture, promoting collaboration and long-term success.

7. Continuous Improvement: The Stoic commitment to self-improvement aligns seamlessly with the entrepreneurial spirit. Business leaders can apply Stoic principles to foster a culture of continuous learning and growth within their organizations. This commitment to improvement contributes not only to the personal development of individuals but also to the overall success and resilience of the business.

Applying Stoic wisdom in business is about translating ancient principles into contemporary leadership practices. By embracing ethical decision-making, cultivating resilience, focusing on the controllable, practicing mindful leadership, maintaining balanced ambition, fostering team collaboration, and committing to continuous improvement, entrepreneurs can create organizations that not only thrive in the marketplace but also contribute positively to the well-being of individuals and society as a whole. Stoicism becomes a guiding philosophy for leaders who seek not just financial success but enduring significance in the impact they make through their businesses.

JANUARY: CLARITY AND VISION

Setting Clear Intentions

In the dynamic landscape of business, setting clear intentions is not just a theoretical concept but a pragmatic strategy that has fueled the success of iconic companies. Apple Inc., under the visionary leadership of Steve Jobs, provides a compelling illustration of how intentional goal-setting can shape the destiny of a business.

When Steve Jobs returned to Apple in 1997, the company was grappling with financial losses and a fragmented product line. Jobs, known for his unwavering focus and commitment to innovation, set a clear intention to redefine Apple's brand and revive its reputation for cutting-edge technology. His first intentional move was streamlining the product portfolio. Jobs axed numerous underperforming products, concentrating the company's efforts on a few core offerings. This intentional simplification not only reduced operational complexity but also allowed Apple to concentrate its resources on creating exceptional products.

The launch of the iPod in 2001 exemplifies Jobs' intentional approach to innovation. With a clear intention to revolutionize the music industry, Jobs envisioned a seamless integration of hardware and software. The iPod became a game-changer, setting the stage for Apple's dominance in the consumer electronics market. Jobs' vision extended beyond individual products to the overall user experience. The launch of the iPhone in 2007 was a testament to his intention to redefine the smartphone industry. The device seamlessly integrated communication, entertainment, and productivity, setting new standards for design and functionality. This intentional move catapulted Apple into a leadership position in the mobile technology space.

Moreover, Jobs' intentional focus on design aesthetics transformed Apple into a lifestyle brand. The intentional choice to prioritize sleek, minimalist design elevated Apple's products beyond mere gadgets to coveted lifestyle accessories. This intentional brand image became a significant driver of consumer loyalty and market dominance. Setting clear intentions also played a pivotal role in Apple's retail strategy. Jobs envisioned Apple stores as more than just sales outlets; they were intentional spaces for customer engagement and brand immersion. The unique store layouts and emphasis on customer experience reflected Jobs' intentional commitment to making every interaction with Apple a memorable one.

The success of Apple Inc., with its groundbreaking products and iconic brand, is a testament to the power of setting clear intentions. Steve Jobs' intentional leadership, characterized by a laser focus on innovation, user experience, and brand aesthetics, has left an indelible mark on the business world. *The Apple paradigm underscores that intentional goal-setting is not only a foundation for strategic decision-making but a catalyst for transformative and sustained success in the competitive landscape of business.*

In the realm of entrepreneurship, where ambiguity and rapid changes are constants, setting clear intentions becomes a guiding principle that aligns actions with purpose and values. Drawing on Stoic philosophy, entrepreneurs can benefit from the practice of delineating precise intentions, offering a roadmap for ethical decision-making, focused leadership, and sustained success.

1. Aligning Actions with Values: Stoicism underscores the importance of living in accordance with one's values. Entrepreneurs who set clear intentions align their actions with ethical principles, creating a foundation for a purpose-driven business. By defining values such as integrity, responsibility, and empathy, entrepreneurs establish a moral compass that guides decision-making and shapes the organizational culture.

2. Defining the Entrepreneurial Vision: Clear intentions serve as the foundation for a well-defined entrepreneurial vision. Stoic philosophy encourages entrepreneurs to contemplate their long-term objectives and the impact they aspire to make. By articulating a vision that transcends immediate financial goals, entrepreneurs infuse their ventures with meaning and purpose, motivating both themselves and their teams.

3. Navigating Decision-Making: In the dynamic landscape of business, decisions can be fraught with complexity and ambiguity. Setting clear intentions provides entrepreneurs with a framework for decision-making. When faced with choices, Stoic-minded entrepreneurs can refer back to their intentions, ensuring that decisions align with the overarching purpose and values they have established for their ventures.

4. Building Resilience: Stoicism teaches that setting intentions is not just about achieving specific outcomes but also about cultivating resilience in the face of challenges. Entrepreneurs who clearly define their intentions are better equipped to persevere through setbacks. Stoic principles guide them to view obstacles as opportunities for growth, fostering a resilient mindset that contributes to long-term success.

5. Enhancing Focus and Productivity: Clarity of intention enhances focus and productivity. Entrepreneurs inundated with myriad tasks and priorities can refer back to their established intentions as a compass for prioritization. This Stoic approach promotes a disciplined focus on what truly matters, reducing distractions and increasing efficiency in the pursuit of overarching goals.

6. Encouraging Team Alignment: Clear intentions serve as a unifying force within an organization. Stoic-minded entrepreneurs communicate their vision and intentions effectively to their teams, fostering alignment and a shared sense of purpose. This shared understanding contributes to a positive and collaborative workplace culture, where every team member is working towards a common goal.

7. Reflection and Adaptation: Stoicism encourages continuous reflection and adaptation. Entrepreneurs setting clear intentions regularly evaluate their progress, reflecting on both successes and challenges. This Stoic practice enables entrepreneurs to adapt their intentions in response to changing circumstances, ensuring that their ventures remain purposeful and aligned with their evolving values.

In the world of entrepreneurship, where the path forward is often uncertain, setting clear intentions becomes a Stoic compass for ethical decision-making, resilient leadership, and purposeful action. By adopting this practice, entrepreneurs cultivate a mindset that transcends immediate challenges, guiding them towards a meaningful and impactful journey in the world of business. Stoic principles, with their emphasis on virtue and purpose, empower entrepreneurs to not only achieve success but to do so with a sense of fulfillment and enduring significance.

Embracing the Power of Choice

In the realm of entrepreneurship, the power of choice is a formidable force that shapes the destiny of businesses and their leaders. Consider the story of Alex Turner, founder and CEO of a tech startup, as an illustration of how embracing the Stoic principle of choice transformed both his decision-making process and the trajectory of his company. In the early stages of his entrepreneurial journey, Alex faced a critical choice that many founders encounter—whether to pivot the business model or stay the course. Faced with mounting challenges and external pressures, he turned to Stoic philosophy for guidance. Recognizing the power of choice as a core Stoic principle, Alex understood that he had control over the decisions he made, even in the face of unpredictable market dynamics.

Aligning his choices with Stoic virtues, Alex made a conscious decision to pivot the business, a move that required courage and strategic vision. Stoicism guided him to overcome the fear of failure and view the pivot not as a setback but as an opportunity for growth and adaptation. This mindset shift influenced not only the trajectory of the business but also the culture within the organization. The power of choice played a pivotal role in shaping Alex's leadership style. He consciously aligned his choices with the core values of the company—transparency, innovation, and customer-centricity. This ethical decision-making not only bolstered the company's reputation but also cultivated a sense of trust and loyalty among employees, fostering a positive workplace culture. As the startup continued to grow, Alex faced the challenge of managing rapid expansion. Stoicism's emphasis on prioritizing what truly matters guided his decision-making. Rather than succumbing to decision fatigue, he focused on choices that aligned with the long-term goals of the company. This mindful approach to decision-making became a strategic asset, enabling the organization to navigate challenges and capitalize on opportunities more effectively. The Stoic perspective also influenced how Alex approached risk. By evaluating risks objectively and aligning decisions with calculated choices, he created a culture that embraced strategic risk-taking. The power of choice, coupled with a Stoic mindset, allowed the company to innovate boldly, positioning itself as an industry leader.

In the face of inevitable setbacks and uncertainties, Alex's journey exemplifies how the power of choice, informed by Stoic wisdom, can transform the narrative of an entrepreneurial venture. By embracing the Stoic principle of choice, entrepreneurs like Alex gain a profound understanding of their ability to shape their destinies, make principled decisions, and navigate the dynamic landscape of business with purpose and resilience.

Aligning Actions with Values

The corporate landscape is replete with stories of businesses that soared to success by aligning their actions with core values. A prime example is the journey of

Johnson & Johnson (J&J), a multinational pharmaceutical and consumer goods company. In 1982, J&J faced a crisis when seven people died after consuming capsules laced with cyanide. This incident could have been a catastrophic blow to the company's reputation, but J&J's response showcased a commitment to aligning actions with values. Upon learning of the tampering, J&J immediately prioritized public safety over profit. In a bold move, the company issued a nationwide recall of 31 million bottles of Tylenol, the product implicated in the deaths, even though the tampering occurred outside their control. This decision, guided by the values of integrity and customer safety, set a new standard for crisis management in the business world. J&J's CEO at the time, James Burke, took a transparent and ethical approach. He communicated openly with the public, the media, and law enforcement agencies, demonstrating the Stoic virtue of courage in the face of adversity. The company also introduced tamper-evident packaging, pioneering a new industry standard to ensure consumer safety.

The strategic alignment of actions with values during this crisis not only salvaged J&J's reputation but enhanced it. The company's commitment to ethical principles and customer well-being was underscored, leading to a swift recovery in market share and a restoration of consumer trust. This commitment to values extended beyond the crisis. J&J continued to prioritize social responsibility, environmental sustainability, and ethical business practices. The company's Credo, a document outlining its core values, became a guiding force for decision-making, from product development to corporate governance. By aligning actions with values, J&J demonstrated that ethical choices can be strategically sound. The company's success story serves as a testament to the enduring impact of prioritizing values over short-term gains. In an era where consumers demand transparency and ethical conduct, J&J's journey showcases the tangible benefits of aligning actions with a strong set of values, both in times of crisis and during the day-to-day operations of a successful business.

Practical exercises for business clarity and vision

Values Clarification:

Exercise: Clearly define your core values as they relate to your business. What principles guide your decisions and actions? Reflect on how these values align with your business vision.

Obstacle Anticipation:

Exercise: Identify potential obstacles or challenges your business may face. Develop strategic plans for addressing each obstacle, emphasizing adaptability and resilience. This exercise helps foster a proactive mindset.

Mission Statement Review:

Exercise: Revisit and refine your business mission statement. Does it accurately reflect your long-term vision and values? Use this exercise to ensure alignment between your mission and overarching goals.

Decision Journaling:

Exercise: Keep a decision journal for business choices. Document the thought process behind each decision, evaluating how well it aligns with your vision. Learn from both successful and unsuccessful outcomes.

Stakeholder Reflection:

Exercise: Consider the impact of your business decisions on stakeholders – employees, customers, and the community. Reflect on how your actions contribute to the well-being of all parties involved.

Customer Empathy Mapping:

Exercise: Create empathy maps for your target customers. Understand their needs, challenges, and aspirations. This exercise enhances clarity on how your business can provide value and align with customer desires.

Strategic Pause:

Exercise: Before initiating a new business strategy, take a strategic pause. Reflect on how the strategy aligns with long-term objectives. Consider potential consequences and whether it reinforces your business vision.

Leadership Virtues Assessment:

Exercise: Evaluate your leadership style against Stoic virtues – wisdom, courage, justice, and temperance. Identify areas for improvement and outline practical steps to align your leadership with Stoic principles.

Innovation and Adaptation Workshop:

Exercise: Host a workshop to encourage innovative thinking and adaptability among your team. Prompt discussions on how new ideas align with the business vision and contribute to long-term goals.

Weekly Vision Check-In:

Exercise: Set aside a weekly session to review your business vision. Assess progress, recalibrate strategies if necessary, and reaffirm your commitment to the overarching goals. This exercise promotes ongoing clarity and alignment.

These Stoic practical exercises are tailored for business leaders seeking clarity and vision in their professional endeavors. By integrating these exercises into the daily operations of a business, leaders can cultivate a Stoic-inspired approach that enhances decision-making, strategic planning, and overall business success.

FEBRUARY: RESILIENCE IN THE FACE OF CHALLENGES

Navigating Uncertainty

In the volatile world of business, where unpredictability is a constant, the Stoic philosophy offers a timeless guide for entrepreneurs and business leaders facing the unpredictable twists and turns of the marketplace. Navigating uncertainty through a Stoic lens involves cultivating resilience, embracing change, and making decisions rooted in wisdom and virtue. One fundamental Stoic principle that aids in navigating uncertainty is the "Dichotomy of Control." Entrepreneurs are encouraged to distinguish between factors within their control and those beyond it. External market fluctuations, economic conditions, and unforeseen challenges fall into the category of the uncontrollable. Stoicism teaches leaders to focus their energy on aspects within their control—strategic decision-making, ethical conduct, and adaptability.

Embracing the philosophy's teachings on impermanence, entrepreneurs are prompted to accept the transient nature of business conditions. The Stoic concept of "Amor Fati," or love of fate, encourages a mindset shift from resisting uncertainty to embracing it as an inherent part of the entrepreneurial journey. By accepting and adapting to change, leaders foster a resilience that enables them to thrive amidst uncertainty rather than be paralyzed by it. Stoicism also emphasizes the power of mindfulness in navigating uncertainty. Leaders are encouraged to be present in the moment, avoiding excessive fixation on past failures or anxious anticipation of future challenges. This mindfulness fosters clarity of thought, enabling leaders to make well-informed decisions in the face of uncertainty.

The Stoic principle of "Premeditatio Malorum," or premeditation of evils, equips entrepreneurs with a practical tool for managing uncertainty. This exercise involves anticipating potential challenges and mentally preparing for them. By envisioning various scenarios, leaders can develop contingency plans and respond to unexpected events with composure rather than panic. Additionally, the Stoic virtue of practical wisdom, or "Phronesis," guides leaders to make rational decisions in the midst of uncertainty. By leveraging informed judgment and strategic thinking, entrepreneurs navigate complex situations with a steady hand. Stoicism encourages leaders to see challenges not as insurmountable obstacles but as opportunities for growth and learning. The story of Marcus Aurelius, a Stoic philosopher and Roman Emperor, serves as an inspiring example of navigating uncertainty with wisdom. Leading during times of political unrest and external threats, Aurelius applied Stoic principles to maintain composure, prioritize virtue, and make decisions aligned with the greater good.

In conclusion, navigating uncertainty in business through a Stoic approach involves cultivating resilience, accepting the impermanence of conditions, practicing mindfulness, and applying practical wisdom. Entrepreneurs who embrace these Stoic principles not only weather uncertainties with greater ease but also transform challenges into opportunities for personal and professional growth. Stoicism becomes a guiding philosophy that empowers leaders to navigate the unpredictable terrain of business with a calm and purposeful mindset.

Turning Obstacles into Opportunities

In the annals of business history, the narrative of Ford Motor Company and its founder, Henry Ford, serves as a vivid example of applying Stoic principles to turn obstacles into opportunities. Facing financial constraints and technological challenges, Ford encountered a pivotal obstacle in the early 20th century—the need for an innovative manufacturing process.

Perception Shift: In embracing Stoic principles, Henry Ford underwent a profound shift in perception. Rather than viewing the obstacle of limited resources as a hindrance, he perceived it as an opportunity to revolutionize manufacturing. Ford's vision was to make automobiles affordable and accessible to the masses, an idea that required a radical rethinking of production methods.

Adaptive Problem-Solving: Ford's response to the obstacle of resource limitations was Stoic-inspired adaptive problem-solving. He introduced the assembly line, a groundbreaking manufacturing process that significantly reduced production time and costs. This innovative solution not only addressed immediate challenges but also transformed the automobile industry by making cars more affordable and ushering in an era of mass production.

Resilience in the Face of Setbacks: Facing setbacks and initial skepticism about his revolutionary approach, Henry Ford exemplified Stoic resilience. Instead of succumbing to doubt, he persevered in refining and implementing the assembly line. This resilience not only propelled Ford Motor Company to success but also established a new standard for efficiency in manufacturing.

Strategic Innovation: Ford's utilization of the assembly line reflected Stoic-inspired strategic innovation. Rather than viewing obstacles as impediments, he strategically innovated to overcome challenges. The assembly line became a cornerstone of Ford's success, setting a precedent for businesses to view obstacles not merely as problems to solve but as opportunities for strategic innovation.

Learning from Adversity: Henry Ford's journey underscores the Stoic principle of learning from adversity. His early failures, including the bankruptcy of his first company, equipped him with invaluable lessons. These setbacks became stepping stones for Ford, shaping his approach to business and contributing to the development of more resilient and adaptive strategies.

Crisis as Catalyst for Change: Ford's story epitomizes the Stoic notion of crises as catalysts for change. The obstacle of financial turmoil and industry challenges acted as a catalyst for Ford's visionary transformation. Instead of succumbing to the crisis, he used it as an opportunity to revolutionize manufacturing and redefine the automobile industry.

Turning Weaknesses into Strengths: Henry Ford's Stoic-inspired mindset involved turning weaknesses into strengths. The limitation of resources and the challenge of making automobiles affordable became the strength of Ford Motor Company. By addressing these weaknesses strategically, Ford not only built a successful business but also revolutionized an entire industry.

In the Stoic-inspired narrative of Ford Motor Company, the principles of perception shift, adaptive problem-solving, resilience, strategic innovation, learning from adversity, crisis as a catalyst, and turning weaknesses into strengths are woven into the fabric of success. By applying these Stoic principles, Henry Ford not only navigated obstacles effectively but also transformed challenges into opportunities that reshaped the business landscape. His story serves as a timeless testament to the enduring relevance of Stoicism in the realm of business.

Building Emotional Resilience

In the corporate landscape, where volatility and unpredictability are constants, the story of Elon Musk and his experiences with Tesla and SpaceX offers a compelling narrative of building emotional resilience inspired by Stoic principles. Facing Criticism and Market Skepticism: In the early 2010s, Tesla faced skepticism from both industry experts and the general public. Elon Musk, the CEO, found himself navigating a barrage of criticism regarding Tesla's viability and market potential. Stoicism guided Musk to view external opinions as beyond his control and focus on his actions and responses.

Perseverance in the Face of Setbacks: As Tesla encountered production delays and technical challenges, Musk exemplified Stoic perseverance. Rather than succumbing to the pressure of setbacks, he maintained a steadfast commitment to the long-term vision of sustainable transportation. This resilience became a hallmark of Musk's leadership as he weathered storms that could have derailed the company.

Adaptive Problem-Solving: Tesla's journey reflects Stoic-inspired adaptive problem-solving. Musk approached challenges with a strategic mindset, seeking innovative solutions. For example, when faced with production bottlenecks, he personally delved into the manufacturing process, identifying inefficiencies and implementing improvements. This hands-on approach demonstrated a Stoic willingness to engage with challenges directly.

Handling Intense Public Scrutiny: Elon Musk's public persona often attracted intense scrutiny and criticism. Stoicism influenced his response to this scrutiny, guiding him to remain emotionally resilient in the face of public pressure. Musk recognized that public opinion was beyond his control and focused on aligning his actions with his convictions, contributing to the Stoic principle of internal locus of control.

Mindful Approach to Success and Failure: Stoicism encourages individuals to approach success and failure with equanimity. When Tesla achieved milestones, Musk maintained a measured perspective, avoiding excessive celebration. Conversely, in times of failure or setbacks, he embraced the Stoic notion that these were opportunities for growth rather than insurmountable obstacles.

Navigating High-Stakes Challenges at SpaceX: The Stoic philosophy also played a crucial role in Musk's leadership at SpaceX. Facing high-stakes challenges in the aerospace industry, including the ambitious goal of making space travel more accessible, Musk embraced Stoic resilience. His ability to confront the potential for failure with a calm determination propelled SpaceX through *uncharted territories.*

Balancing Stoicism and Passion: Elon Musk's journey embodies the Stoic principle of balancing rationality with passion. While Stoicism guided him to maintain emotional resilience in turbulent times, Musk's unwavering passion for transformative innovation remained the driving force behind his actions. This synthesis of Stoic principles and entrepreneurial zeal underscored the capacity to build emotional resilience while pursuing audacious goals.

The story of Elon Musk's leadership at Tesla and SpaceX is a factual illustration of building emotional resilience inspired by Stoic philosophy. Musk's ability to navigate criticism, persevere in the face of setbacks, engage in adaptive problem-solving, handle public scrutiny, approach success and failure mindfully, and balance Stoicism with passion exemplifies how Stoic principles can be applied in the dynamic and challenging realm of business leadership.

Practical exercises for Resilience in the face of challenge

Stoic Reflection on Control:

Exercise: List factors within your control and those beyond control in your current business situation. Focus your energy on actionable items, fostering a Stoic mindset that empowers you to navigate challenges strategically.

Anticipate Obstacles:

Exercise: Conduct a proactive analysis of potential obstacles your business may face. Develop contingency plans for each scenario, incorporating Stoic principles of preparedness and adaptability.

Virtue-Centered Decision Journal:

Exercise: Keep a journal documenting decisions made during challenging situations. Reflect on how each decision aligns with Stoic virtues such as wisdom, courage, justice, and temperance. Use this practice to reinforce ethical decision-making.

Daily Affirmations of Resilience:

Exercise: Create daily affirmations centered around resilience. Affirm Stoic principles of enduring challenges, learning from adversity, and maintaining composure in the face of uncertainty. Repeat these affirmations to reinforce a resilient mindset.

Obstacle-to-Opportunity Mapping:

Exercise: When faced with a challenge, map out potential opportunities that may arise from overcoming it. This exercise encourages a Stoic perspective of transforming obstacles into strategic advantages.

Resilience Through Team Values:

Exercise: Collaborate with your team to define core values that promote resilience. Discuss how these values can guide collective responses to challenges, fostering a resilient organizational culture aligned with Stoic principles.

Adaptive Leadership Workshop:

Exercise: Facilitate a workshop focused on adaptive leadership. Encourage team members to share strategies for adapting to change and uncertainty. Draw parallels with Stoic philosophy to emphasize the importance of adaptability in challenging times.

Mindful Decision Pause:

Exercise: When faced with a critical decision, implement a Stoic-inspired pause. Take a few minutes for mindful reflection, considering the decision's alignment with long-term goals and Stoic principles. This practice encourages thoughtful decision-making under pressure.

Stoic Mindfulness Meditation:

Exercise: Integrate Stoic mindfulness meditation into your routine. Focus on the present moment, acknowledging thoughts without attachment. This practice enhances emotional regulation and resilience in the face of business challenges.

Learning from Setbacks Review:

Exercise: Regularly conduct a review of setbacks and challenges your business has faced. Identify key lessons learned, emphasizing the Stoic principle of viewing adversity as a source of wisdom. Use these insights to inform future decision-making and organizational resilience.

These practical exercises and prompts are designed to cultivate resilience in the face of business challenges, drawing inspiration from Stoic philosophy. Consistent engagement with these exercises can contribute to the development of a resilient mindset, adaptive leadership, and a purpose-driven approach to overcoming obstacles in the dynamic landscape of business.

MARCH: LEADERSHIP AND INFLUENCE

Leading with Virtue

In the realm of business leadership, the narrative of Mary Barra, the CEO of General Motors (GM), serves as a factual exemplar of leading with virtue, drawing inspiration from Stoic philosophy. Barra's leadership journey at GM reflects a commitment to Stoic virtues—wisdom, courage, justice, and temperance—as guiding principles for ethical decision-making.

Wisdom in Strategic Vision: Mary Barra's tenure at GM is marked by strategic wisdom. Adopting a Stoic approach, she navigated complex industry challenges with a forward-thinking vision. Rather than succumbing to short-term pressures, Barra's strategic decisions exemplify the Stoic virtue of wisdom, aligning actions with the long-term success and sustainability of the company.

Courage in Crisis Management: The Stoic virtue of courage is evident in Barra's handling of the ignition switch crisis that unfolded in 2014. Confronted with a significant challenge that impacted safety and trust in the brand, Barra exhibited moral courage. She took responsibility, initiated transparent communication, and implemented necessary changes to address the issue—a testament to Stoic courage in the face of adversity.

Justice in Organizational Culture: Leading with justice, Barra prioritized a culture of accountability and fairness within GM. The Stoic virtue of justice guided her commitment to addressing issues of workplace misconduct and promoting a culture of inclusion. Barra's dedication to justice extends beyond legal compliance, emphasizing a moral responsibility to create an ethical and equitable work environment.

Temperance in Executive Compensation: Barra's leadership at GM reflects the Stoic virtue of temperance, particularly in the realm of executive compensation. In response to shareholder concerns, she demonstrated restraint and moderation, aligning executive pay with the company's performance. This Stoic-inspired approach reflects a commitment to ethical and temperate decision-making in the context of corporate governance.

Learning from Adversity and Humility: Stoicism emphasizes learning from adversity and practicing humility. Barra's response to the ignition switch crisis showcases these Stoic principles. Rather than deflecting blame, she embraced a learning mindset, acknowledging mistakes and demonstrating humility. This approach fosters a culture of continuous improvement and resilience in the face of challenges.

Balancing Stakeholder Interests: Leading with virtue involves balancing the interests of various stakeholders. Barra's leadership is characterized by a commitment to stakeholders beyond shareholders, including employees, customers, and communities. This Stoic-inspired approach aligns with the virtue of justice, ensuring a balanced consideration of diverse interests in decision-making.

Mary Barra's leadership at General Motors provides a factual narrative of leading with virtue in the business world, drawing inspiration from Stoic principles. Her strategic wisdom, courage in crisis, commitment to justice, temperance in decision-making, humility in adversity, and balanced stakeholder approach collectively exemplify how Stoicism can serve as a pragmatic guide for ethical leadership in the complex landscape of modern business. Barra's journey reinforces that leading with virtue is not just an aspirational ideal but a tangible blueprint for sustained business success and ethical corporate governance.

Inspiring and Motivating Teams

Elon Musk's leadership at SpaceX and Tesla provides a factual illustration of inspiring and motivating teams in the domains of innovation and technology. Musk intertwines Stoic principles with a visionary approach, creating a narrative of leadership that transcends traditional paradigms. Musk's commitment to transformative goals and persistent pursuit of objectives serves as a potent source of inspiration for teams. From overcoming the early struggles of SpaceX to addressing production challenges at Tesla, Musk's Stoic-inspired perseverance becomes a driving force, fostering resilience within his teams. Transparent communication, marked by clarity and directness, is a cornerstone of Musk's leadership. Openly sharing challenges, progress, and objectives ensures that teams are well-informed and aligned with the overarching vision. This transparency builds trust and shared responsibility, motivating teams to work cohesively towards common goals.

Musk's practice of acknowledging and celebrating team achievements serves as motivational markers. Public recognition of successful rocket launches or production milestones reinforces the significance of collective efforts, instilling a sense of pride and accomplishment among team members. Fostering a culture of innovation and autonomy, Musk empowers teams to explore creative solutions and take ownership of their work. This approach aligns with Stoic principles, recognizing that individuals find fulfillment in contributing meaningfully to collective goals. Musk's personal dedication to the missions of SpaceX and Tesla serves as a powerful source of inspiration. Leading by example, he actively engages in intricate engineering challenges and dedicates long hours to his work, motivating teams to match his level of commitment.

In the factual narrative of Elon Musk's leadership, the synthesis of visionary pursuits with Stoic-inspired values is evident. Musk's commitment to transformative goals, transparent communication, celebration of achievements, empowerment of teams, and personal dedication collectively form a leadership style that not only propels technological innovation but also inspires teams to engage in extraordinary endeavors.

Effective Communication in Business

In the realm of corporate leadership, the story of Marcus Aurelius, the Stoic Roman Emperor, serves as a factual narrative on the significance of effective communication.

While not a contemporary business figure, Aurelius' principles have timeless relevance, and his leadership during the Roman Empire offers valuable insights into the Stoic-inspired approach to communication.

Clarity and Stoic Wisdom: Aurelius, known for his clarity of thought and adherence to Stoic philosophy, exemplified the importance of clear communication. In his meditations, he emphasized the need for leaders to articulate their vision with simplicity and precision. By distilling complex ideas into straightforward messages, Aurelius ensured that his soldiers and administrators understood the overarching goals of the empire, fostering unity and purpose.

Empathy and Stoic Virtue: Stoicism places great emphasis on virtues such as empathy. Aurelius, while leading a vast empire, exhibited empathy in his communications. He acknowledged the challenges faced by different segments of society and strove to address their concerns. This Stoic virtue of understanding and resonating with the experiences of others contributed to a more cohesive and harmonious Roman Empire.

Strategic Storytelling and Stoic Wisdom: Aurelius, in his reflective writings, often employed strategic storytelling to convey philosophical lessons. Stoicism values the use of anecdotes and parables to impart wisdom. Similarly, leaders in the business world can draw inspiration from Aurelius by incorporating strategic storytelling into their communication strategies, making complex concepts more relatable and inspiring.

Open Dialogue and Stoic Principles: The Stoic philosophy encourages open dialogue and rational discourse. Aurelius embraced this principle by engaging in conversations with his advisors, philosophers, and even common citizens. By fostering an environment of open communication, he gained valuable insights, and his decisions were informed by a diversity of perspectives—a Stoic-inspired approach that can be adapted in contemporary business leadership.

Crisis Communication with Stoic Resilience: Aurelius faced numerous crises during his rule, including military conflicts and internal challenges. His Stoic resilience was evident in his communication during these turbulent times. Instead of succumbing to panic, he communicated with composure and determination, instilling confidence in the face of adversity. This Stoic approach to crisis communication is a valuable lesson for leaders navigating challenges in the business arena.

Cultural Sensitivity and Stoic Wisdom: Leading an empire with diverse cultures, Aurelius understood the importance of cultural sensitivity. He communicated in a way that respected the unique traditions and values of different regions. This Stoic-inspired cultural awareness contributed to a sense of unity within the Roman Empire—a lesson for modern leaders navigating the complexities of a globalized business environment.

In the Stoic-inspired narrative of Marcus Aurelius, effective communication emerges as a foundational pillar of successful leadership. His commitment to clarity, empathy, strategic storytelling, open dialogue, crisis communication, and cultural sensitivity serves as a Stoic guide for contemporary leaders striving to navigate the complexities of the business landscape with wisdom and resilience.

In the realm of modern business, the leadership of Alan Mulally, former CEO of Ford, exemplifies the impact of effective communication rooted in Stoic principles. When Mulally took the reins in 2006, he faced a company in crisis. His Stoic-inspired clarity of vision, communicated through a unified message of innovation and financial stability, became a rallying point for Ford's teams. Mulally's empathetic approach, fostering open dialogue through weekly meetings, cultivated a culture of mutual understanding and teamwork. Drawing on Stoic traditions, he used strategic storytelling to convey the urgency of Ford's situation, aligning employees with a collective commitment to the company's turnaround. His commitment to transparent communication during the 2008 financial crisis instilled confidence and positioned Ford for success. Stoically resilient, Mulally navigated challenges with candor and implemented measures that secured the company's future.

Navigating a global business landscape, Mulally's cultural sensitivity was evident in a communication strategy that respected diverse perspectives. In the Stoic-inspired narrative of Mulally's leadership, effective communication emerges as a linchpin for organizational success, showcasing how Stoic principles can guide leaders through challenges with wisdom and resilience.

Practical exercises for leadership and influence

Reflect on Virtues:

Exercise: Regularly contemplate Stoic virtues such as wisdom, courage, justice, and temperance. Evaluate your leadership decisions against these virtues, striving to align your actions with ethical principles.

Morning Meditation on Goals:

Exercise: Begin each day with a Stoic-inspired meditation. Reflect on your leadership goals, visualizing how you can embody Stoic virtues to influence and lead effectively throughout the day.

Negative Visualization for Resilience:

Exercise: Practice negative visualization by imagining potential challenges and setbacks in your business. This Stoic exercise helps you build resilience and prepares you to respond effectively in the face of adversity.

Practice Silence and Listening:

Exercise: Embrace the Stoic concept of "saying less and listening more." During meetings, focus on active listening without immediately responding. This cultivates a thoughtful and measured approach to communication.

Control Assessment:

Exercise: Regularly assess situations based on the Stoic dichotomy of control. Identify factors within your control as a leader and those beyond it. Concentrate your energy on influencing what you can control and accepting what you cannot.

Stoic Journaling for Decision-Making:

Exercise: Maintain a Stoic journal to document your leadership decisions. Reflect on how Stoic principles guided your choices and what lessons you can extract from each situation to enhance your influence and leadership skills.

Daily Virtue Affirmations:

Exercise: Create daily affirmations centered on Stoic virtues. Affirm your commitment to embody wisdom, courage, justice, and temperance in your leadership role, reinforcing these virtues as guiding principles.

Seneca's Pre-Meditatio Malorum:

Exercise: Adopt Seneca's "pre-meditation of evils" by mentally preparing for potential challenges in your leadership journey. This Stoic exercise helps you maintain composure and make sound decisions in the face of adversity.

Role Model Reflection:

Exercise: Identify a historical or contemporary leader whose qualities align with Stoic principles. Reflect on specific actions or decisions they made, and consider how you can incorporate similar virtues into your own leadership style.

Feedback Analysis:

Exercise: Periodically conduct a feedback analysis by seeking input from your team and stakeholders. Embrace constructive criticism and evaluate how Stoic principles can guide you in addressing areas for improvement, fostering continuous growth in your leadership influence.

These practical Stoic exercises and prompts for leadership and influence in business are designed to help leaders integrate Stoic philosophy into their daily practices, fostering resilience, ethical decision-making, and effective influence in the dynamic world of business.

APRIL: TIME MANAGEMENT AND PRODUCTIVITY

Prioritizing the Important

In the fast-paced world of business, leaders often face a myriad of tasks and responsibilities vying for attention. The Stoic philosophy, with its emphasis on discerning the truly important from the superficial, offers valuable insights for leaders seeking to prioritize effectively and lead with purpose. Stoicism encourages leaders to focus on what is within their control, aligning with the principle of "dichotomy of control." This involves distinguishing between aspects one can influence and those beyond one's control. By concentrating efforts on the controllable, leaders can direct their energy toward initiatives that truly matter, fostering a sense of clarity and purpose. A practical Stoic exercise for prioritization involves daily reflection on the overarching goals and values of the organization. Leaders can contemplate the virtues of wisdom, courage, justice, and temperance—Stoic principles that guide decision-making. By consistently aligning actions with these virtues, leaders ensure that their priorities are grounded in ethical considerations, contributing to the long-term success and reputation of the business. Seneca's concept of "pre-meditation of evils" provides a Stoic strategy for anticipating challenges and setbacks. Leaders can engage in scenario planning, envisioning potential obstacles that may arise. This proactive approach allows for strategic preparation and enables leaders to prioritize preemptive actions, contributing to a more resilient and adaptable organization.

Effective prioritization also involves setting clear boundaries. The Stoic practice of "saying less and listening more" underscores the importance of active listening and thoughtful communication. By discerning the most critical issues and actively engaging with stakeholders, leaders can prioritize their time and resources on matters of true significance. Stoic journaling serves as a reflective tool for leaders to assess and prioritize their daily tasks. Recording decisions and their outcomes allows leaders to identify patterns, refine their priorities, and continuously improve their decision-making processes. This journaling exercise aligns with the Stoic commitment to self-awareness and ongoing personal development. In the Stoic narrative, the Roman Emperor Marcus Aurelius serves as an exemplar of prioritizing the important. Despite the vast responsibilities of leading an empire, Aurelius prioritized the well-being of his subjects, embodying Stoic virtues in his decision-making. His focus on ethical leadership and prioritizing the welfare of the Roman people reflects the enduring impact of prioritizing the truly important in the face of myriad responsibilities.

In essence, the Stoic philosophy provides a timeless framework for leaders to navigate the complexities of prioritization. By embracing the dichotomy of control, contemplating virtues, pre-meditating potential challenges, setting boundaries, and engaging in reflective practices, leaders can prioritize the important with clarity, purpose, and resilience in the ever-evolving landscape of business.

Embracing the Power of Focus

In the dynamic and competitive landscape of business, the ability to embrace the power of focus is a hallmark of effective leadership. Drawing insights from successful leaders and Stoic philosophy, this factual exploration sheds light on how prioritizing focus contributes to strategic decision-making, heightened productivity, and long-term organizational success. One notable figure illustrating the power of focus is Steve Jobs, co-founder of Apple Inc. Jobs, renowned for his visionary leadership, exemplified the impact of unwavering focus on key priorities. His deliberate approach to product development, epitomized by the singular focus on creating groundbreaking innovations like the iPhone, illustrates the potency of concentrating efforts on a few pivotal initiatives. Stoicism, with its emphasis on the "dichotomy of control," aligns seamlessly with the concept of focus in leadership. Leaders practicing Stoicism recognize the importance of distinguishing between factors they can control and those beyond their influence. By directing attention and resources toward controllable elements, leaders foster a sense of focus that is crucial for navigating challenges and achieving meaningful outcomes.

Practicing the Stoic exercise of negative visualization further reinforces the power of focus. By contemplating potential setbacks and challenges, leaders prepare themselves mentally and strategically for various scenarios. This Stoic-inspired foresight enables a more focused and proactive approach, contributing to agile decision-making in the face of uncertainty. Effective leaders often leverage the power of focus through strategic goal-setting. The Stoic principle of reflecting on virtues, such as wisdom and temperance, aligns with the process of setting clear and meaningful objectives. This clarity of purpose serves as a guiding beacon, allowing leaders and their teams to align their efforts toward shared goals and aspirations. In the Stoic narrative, the Roman Emperor Marcus Aurelius provides a historical illustration of focus in leadership. Despite the vast responsibilities of ruling an empire, Aurelius maintained a disciplined focus on Stoic virtues and the well-being of his subjects. This unwavering commitment to priorities showcases the enduring impact of focus on ethical leadership and organizational success. Moreover, studies on workplace productivity consistently emphasize the importance of focus. Research indicates that multitasking can lead to reduced efficiency and increased errors. Leaders who cultivate a culture of focus within their teams contribute to a more productive and innovative work environment, fostering collective success.

In conclusion, embracing the power of focus is not only a timeless principle illustrated by impactful leaders like Steve Jobs and Marcus Aurelius but is also supported by empirical evidence in the realm of workplace productivity. By aligning with Stoic philosophy, leaders can harness the potency of focus to make strategic decisions, enhance productivity, and steer their organizations toward sustained success in the competitive landscape of business.

Mastering the Art of Saying "No"

In the corridors of modern business lore, the narrative of Steve Jobs, co-founder and visionary leader of Apple Inc., serves as a compelling tale illustrating the profound impact of mastering the art of saying "no." Jobs, renowned for his transformative influence on the technology industry, strategically wielded this two-letter word to shape Apple's trajectory into a global powerhouse. Amid the myriad challenges and opportunities that confronted

Apple during its resurgence in the late 1990s, Jobs demonstrated an unyielding commitment to focus and simplicity. One pivotal moment encapsulates this strategic saying of "no" – the decision to streamline Apple's product line. Jobs, with Stoic-like clarity, eliminated a plethora of underperforming products, choosing to concentrate on a select few that would redefine industries. The introduction of the iPod, iPhone, and iPad under Jobs' leadership showcased the power of saying "no" to distractions and non-essential ventures. By refusing to dilute Apple's innovation with a plethora of mediocre products, Jobs focused the company's creative energy, resulting in groundbreaking, industry-shaping devices that propelled Apple to unprecedented success.

Jobs' approach to saying "no" extended beyond product lines. He strategically declined partnerships and ventures that did not align with Apple's core values and design philosophy. This disciplined refusal contributed to the company's distinctive brand identity and unwavering commitment to delivering exceptional user experiences. The Stoic-inspired lesson embedded in Jobs' business journey is clear – the art of saying "no" is not a mere rejection; it is a deliberate, strategic tool. By strategically refusing opportunities that diverge from the core vision, leaders can sculpt a focused, purposeful trajectory for their organizations, much like Jobs did with Apple.

In the evolving landscape of business, Jobs' strategic saying of "no" stands as a testament to the transformative power of this seemingly simple word. It echoes the timeless wisdom of Stoicism, illustrating how leaders can navigate complexity and uncertainty by embracing the art of saying "no" strategically, forging a path toward innovation, excellence, and enduring success.

Practical exercises for Time Management and Productivity

Priority Matrix:

Exercise: Begin each day by creating a priority matrix. Identify and categorize tasks into urgent and important, important but not urgent, urgent but not important, and neither urgent nor important. This exercise, inspired by the Eisenhower Matrix, helps you focus on high-priority tasks.

Time Blocking:

Exercise: Implement time blocking by allocating specific blocks of time to different tasks or categories of work. This helps create dedicated periods for focused work and minimizes multitasking, enhancing overall productivity.

Pomodoro Technique:

Exercise: Embrace the Pomodoro Technique by working in focused, 25-minute intervals followed by a 5-minute break. After completing four cycles, take a longer break. This method promotes sustained concentration and prevents burnout.

Batch Processing:

Exercise: Group similar tasks together and tackle them during designated time slots. For instance, respond to emails during specific intervals rather than sporadically throughout the day. Batch processing reduces mental switching and improves efficiency.

Goal Setting and Visualization:

Exercise: Set clear, measurable goals for the day or week. Visualize the successful completion of these goals before starting work. This practice enhances motivation and provides a clear direction for your time management efforts.

Weekly Reviews:

Exercise: Conduct a weekly review to assess completed tasks, evaluate progress toward goals, and adjust priorities for the upcoming week. This reflective practice allows for continuous improvement in time management strategies.

Distraction Journaling:

Exercise: Keep a journal noting instances of distractions throughout the day. Analyze patterns and identify common sources of distraction. Use this awareness to implement strategies to minimize interruptions and maintain focus.

Task Batching:

Exercise: Group similar types of work together to create task batches. For example, dedicate specific time slots for meetings, creative work, and administrative tasks. This minimizes cognitive load associated with context switching.

Digital Detox Periods:

Exercise: Designate specific periods during the day for a digital detox. Turn off non-essential notifications and avoid checking emails or social media. This practice reduces digital distractions and fosters deep work.

Reflection and Adjustment:

Exercise: End each day with a brief reflection on what went well and areas for improvement in time management. Adjust your approach accordingly for the following day, incorporating lessons learned to enhance overall productivity.

These practical exercises and prompts for business time management and productivity aim to provide actionable strategies inspired by proven techniques. By incorporating these practices into your routine, you can cultivate effective time management habits, boost productivity, and achieve a more balanced and focused work life.

MAY: ADAPTABILITY AND INNOVATION

Embracing Change

The evolution of business demands a dynamic response to change, a principle epitomized by the transformative leadership of Satya Nadella at Microsoft. In 2014, Nadella assumed the role of CEO with a commitment to embracing change as a strategic imperative rather than an obstacle. Nadella's approach to change was deeply rooted in the philosophy of a growth mindset. This Stoic-inspired perspective encouraged Microsoft's workforce to view challenges not as roadblocks but as opportunities for learning and innovation. By fostering a culture where change was not just tolerated but embraced, Nadella paved the way for Microsoft to reposition itself as a leader in cloud services. The acquisition of GitHub and LinkedIn exemplifies Microsoft's proactive approach to change. Rather than clinging to established norms, the company recognized the evolving nature of collaboration and professional networking. These strategic acquisitions underscored Microsoft's commitment to adapting to industry shifts and leveraging change as a catalyst for growth.

Nadella's leadership echoes the Stoic principle of "Amor Fati," or love of fate. Instead of fearing disruption, Microsoft actively sought it. The company cultivated a culture where employees not only adapted to change but actively sought opportunities to drive it, embodying a resilient and forward-thinking organizational mindset.

Practical exercises inspired by Microsoft's journey toward embracing change include fostering a growth mindset within your team. Encourage continuous learning, view challenges as opportunities for improvement, and celebrate innovation. Additionally, periodically assess your business model and industry landscape, identifying areas where adaptation is essential for sustained relevance. Embracing change requires a willingness to experiment and pivot when necessary. Develop a culture that values experimentation and learning from failures, aligning with Stoic principles of resilience in the face of setbacks. Create an environment where employees feel empowered to contribute innovative ideas and drive positive change within the organization. Reflecting on past successes and failures is another Stoic-inspired exercise for embracing change. Use these reflections to refine strategies, adjust to evolving market dynamics, and ensure that your business remains agile and adaptable. Celebrate successes as learning milestones and utilize setbacks as opportunities for growth and improvement.

In conclusion, the strategic imperative of embracing change, as exemplified by Satya Nadella's leadership at Microsoft, underscores the importance of cultivating a growth mindset, proactively seeking opportunities in disruption, and fostering a culture of resilience and innovation. These principles serve as a blueprint for navigating change in the ever-evolving landscape of business.

Cultivating a Growth Mindset

The journey of Amazon and its founder, Jeff Bezos, stands as a testament to the transformative power of cultivating a growth mindset within the realm of business leadership. From its humble beginnings as an online bookstore to evolving into a global e-commerce and technology giant, Amazon's success is deeply intertwined with Bezos's commitment to continuous learning, adaptability, and embracing challenges as opportunities. Bezos's approach to cultivating a growth mindset involves viewing setbacks not as failures but as integral parts of the learning process. This Stoic-inspired perspective aligns with the belief that challenges are stepping stones to improvement and innovation. In Amazon's early days, Bezos faced numerous challenges, including skepticism from investors and operational hurdles. Instead of succumbing to these obstacles, he embraced them, viewing each challenge as a chance to refine and strengthen the company's strategies. A practical exercise inspired by Amazon's growth mindset is the implementation of a "failure debrief" within your organization. Encourage team members to share experiences of setbacks, analyze what went wrong, and identify lessons learned. By reframing failure as an opportunity for growth, this exercise fosters a culture where challenges are not feared but embraced as crucial components of the learning journey.

Bezos's emphasis on long-term thinking is another facet of cultivating a growth mindset. Instead of focusing solely on immediate gains, Amazon consistently invested in innovation and expansion, even at the expense of short-term profitability. This forward-thinking approach aligns with Stoic principles of enduring patience and a focus on continuous improvement over time. To cultivate a growth mindset, leaders can also implement a mentorship program within their organizations. Pairing less experienced employees with seasoned mentors provides a platform for knowledge transfer, skill development, and the encouragement of a growth-oriented perspective. Bezos himself valued mentorship and sought guidance from business leaders like Warren Buffett during critical junctures in Amazon's growth. Reflective practices, inspired by Stoicism, play a pivotal role in cultivating a growth mindset. Regularly encourage team members to reflect on their experiences, acknowledge areas for improvement, and set goals for continuous learning. This self-awareness fosters adaptability and a willingness to embrace change within the organizational culture.

In conclusion, the evolution of Amazon under Jeff Bezos's leadership highlights the transformative impact of cultivating a growth mindset. By reframing challenges as opportunities, valuing long-term thinking, promoting mentorship, and embracing reflective practices, leaders can instill a growth mindset within their organizations. This mindset becomes the cornerstone of resilience, adaptability, and sustained success in the ever-changing landscape of business.

Fostering Innovation in Business

In the dynamic landscape of business, fostering innovation is not just a competitive advantage but a fundamental necessity for staying relevant and thriving. Apple Inc., under the leadership of Steve Jobs, serves as a compelling factual narrative illustrating the transformative power of fostering innovation as a core business strategy. Jobs, known for his visionary approach, reshaped industries by fostering a culture of relentless innovation at Apple. One of the key elements of Apple's success lies in its commitment to design thinking and user-centric innovation. The creation of groundbreaking products like the iPod, iPhone, and iPad exemplifies the company's dedication to anticipating and meeting consumer needs through continuous creative exploration. Practical exercises inspired by Apple's paradigm of fostering innovation include encouraging a culture of curiosity and exploration within your organization. Provide employees with the freedom to experiment, take risks, and pursue innovative ideas. Allocate dedicated time for creative thinking and brainstorming sessions, fostering an environment where new ideas can flourish. Implement a cross-functional collaboration model, breaking down silos and encouraging diverse perspectives. Apple's interdisciplinary approach, bringing together designers, engineers, and marketers, resulted in seamless integration of hardware and software, setting new industry standards. This collaborative structure allows for a holistic approach to problem-solving and innovation. Promote a customer-centric mindset by actively seeking and valuing customer feedback. Jobs' obsession with user experience and his famous commitment to giving customers what they didn't know they wanted highlight the importance of staying attuned to evolving market needs. Regularly engage with customers, conduct surveys, and leverage feedback loops to inform and guide innovation efforts. Invest in talent development and continuous learning. Apple's success is not only attributed to Jobs' vision but also to the collective expertise of a talented team. Encourage professional growth through training programs, mentorship, and exposure to diverse perspectives. A commitment to cultivating a skilled and knowledgeable workforce is integral to fostering sustained innovation.

In conclusion, the Apple paradigm of fostering innovation under Steve Jobs provides a factual narrative on the transformative impact of making innovation a core tenet of business strategy. By nurturing a culture of curiosity, promoting cross-functional collaboration, adopting a customer-centric mindset, and investing in talent development, organizations can emulate Apple's success and navigate the ever-evolving business landscape with agility and ingenuity.

Practical exercises for Adaptability and Innovation

Scenario Planning Workshops:

Exercise: Conduct regular scenario planning workshops where teams explore potential future challenges and disruptions. Encourage participants to brainstorm adaptive strategies and innovative solutions to navigate uncertainties.

Cross-Functional Collaboration Days:

Exercise: Designate specific days for cross-functional collaboration, bringing together employees from different departments to work on joint projects. This exercise fosters diverse perspectives, encourages information sharing, and stimulates innovation through interdisciplinary collaboration.

Innovation Sprints:

Exercise: Implement short-term innovation sprints, challenging teams to generate quick and impactful solutions to specific business challenges. Time constraints encourage creative thinking and the rapid development of adaptive strategies.

Customer Feedback Jams:

Exercise: Host regular sessions dedicated to gathering and analyzing customer feedback. Use this information to identify areas for improvement and spark innovation in product development, services, or overall customer experience.

Learning from Failure Sessions:

Exercise: Create a safe space for teams to openly discuss and learn from failures. Analyze past setbacks, identify root causes, and explore innovative approaches to prevent similar challenges in the future. This exercise fosters adaptability and resilience.

Adaptive Leadership Training:

Exercise: Provide training programs focused on adaptive leadership. Equip leaders with tools and strategies to navigate change effectively, inspire innovation, and lead teams through uncertain times.

Future Trends Research Assignments:

Exercise: Assign teams or individuals the task of researching emerging trends in the industry. Encourage them to present their findings and propose innovative strategies for adapting to or leveraging these trends for business growth.

Hackathons for Innovation:

Exercise: Organize hackathons focused on solving specific business challenges. These events bring together employees from various departments to collaborate intensively, fostering a culture of rapid innovation and adaptability.

Adaptability Self-Assessment:

Exercise: Develop a self-assessment tool for employees to evaluate their adaptability skills. Encourage individuals to reflect on their strengths and areas for improvement, providing resources and training opportunities to enhance adaptive capabilities.

Innovation Champions Program:

Exercise: Establish an "Innovation Champions" program where employees passionate about innovation and adaptability lead initiatives within their teams. Empower these champions to spearhead projects, share best practices, and inspire a culture of continuous innovation.

These practical exercises and prompts for business adaptability and innovation are designed to instill a proactive and dynamic approach to change. By integrating these activities into the organizational culture, businesses can cultivate adaptability and foster a mindset that embraces innovation as a strategic imperative.

JUNE: MINDFULNESS AND STRESS MANAGEMENT

Practicing Daily Mindfulness

In the vast and often tumultuous landscape of corporate endeavors, the practice of daily mindfulness emerges not merely as a routine but as a profound navigational tool. Within this narrative, the footsteps of Adobe's leadership, particularly CEO Shantanu Narayen, reveal a factual journey marked by the intentional incorporation of mindfulness practices into the fabric of the organization. Adobe's foray into mindfulness was not a mere trend but a strategic move to enhance creativity, focus, and overall workplace well-being. Narayen, recognizing the demands of the tech industry, championed mindfulness initiatives, including guided meditation sessions and mindfulness workshops. This commitment to fostering a mindful workplace echoes Stoic principles of intentional living and conscious decision-making. Practical exercises inspired by Adobe's approach to daily mindfulness include the introduction of mindfulness breaks throughout the workday. Encourage employees to step away briefly for moments of reflection, deep breathing, or guided meditation. Such deliberate pauses align with Stoic philosophy, emphasizing the importance of intentional breaks to maintain mental clarity and composure. Implement mindfulness training programs to equip employees with tools for stress management and enhanced focus. Adobe's emphasis on cultivating emotional intelligence and resilience resonates with Stoic principles, promoting the idea that a balanced and centered mindset contributes to effective decision-making even in the face of challenges. Encourage a culture of mindful leadership, where executives and managers exemplify intentional and present leadership styles. Adobe's leadership under Narayen reflects a commitment to open communication and empathetic leadership—values in alignment with Stoic ideals of wisdom and compassion in decision-making. Promote the use of mindfulness apps or tools to support daily practice. Whether through technology-assisted meditation or mindful reminders, these resources can help employees integrate mindfulness seamlessly into their daily routines. This practice aligns with Stoic principles by fostering a deeper connection to the present moment and intentional decision-making.

In conclusion, the narrative of Adobe's journey under Shantanu Narayen underscores the transformative impact of daily mindfulness in the corporate realm. By infusing mindfulness into the organizational culture, businesses can empower their workforce with a compass of clarity and resilience, navigating the complexities of the corporate landscape with a steadfast commitment to well-being and intentional living.

Balancing Ambition and Well-being

Embarking on the ambitious journey of corporate success often brings to light the delicate balancing act between ambition and well-being. In the tapestry of this narrative, the story of IBM unfolds, and its former CEO, Ginni Rometty, serves as a beacon illustrating the art of navigating the fine line between professional ambition and personal well-being. Rometty's tenure at IBM was marked by a commitment to fostering a corporate culture that recognized the intrinsic link between employee well-being and sustained success. Her approach was grounded in the belief that an organization's ambitions could not flourish without a workforce that prioritizes mental and physical health. This Stoic-inspired philosophy aligns with the understanding that a sound mind contributes to effective decision-making and sustained excellence. Practical exercises inspired by IBM's approach to balancing ambition and well-being include the promotion of flexible work arrangements. Encourage employees to find a harmonious equilibrium by allowing flexibility in work hours or remote work options. This flexibility echoes Stoic principles, recognizing the importance of adaptability in the pursuit of both personal and professional goals.

Implement well-being programs that prioritize mental health and stress management. IBM's initiatives, such as mindfulness and resilience training, highlight the significance of equipping employees with tools to navigate the challenges inherent in ambitious pursuits. These programs align with Stoic philosophy by fostering a resilient mindset in the face of adversity. Encourage a culture that values regular breaks and time for rejuvenation. Rometty's leadership at IBM underscored the importance of brief respites to recharge creative energies. Stoic principles advocate for intentional pauses, recognizing that periods of rest contribute to enhanced focus and well-being, vital components in the pursuit of ambitious goals. Promote leadership styles that emphasize empathy and holistic success. Rometty's approach to leadership embraced the idea that ambitious goals could be achieved while nurturing a compassionate workplace. This aligns with Stoic ideals of wisdom and benevolence, recognizing that true success encompasses both professional achievements and the well-being of individuals. Acknowledge and celebrate milestones, not only in terms of professional achievements but also in personal growth and well-being. Establish a culture where accomplishments, both big and small, are recognized and celebrated. Stoic philosophy encourages reflection on one's journey, emphasizing the importance of appreciating progress in the pursuit of long-term aspirations.

In conclusion, the narrative of IBM under Ginni Rometty's leadership underscores the imperative of balancing ambition with well-being in the corporate arena. By incorporating practical exercises that prioritize flexibility, mental health, intentional breaks, empathetic leadership, and holistic success, organizations can forge a path where ambition and well-being coalesce. In the symphony of corporate endeavors, achieving harmony between professional aspirations and personal well-being becomes the key to sustained success and fulfillment.

Techniques for Stress Reduction

In the relentless pursuit of professional success within the corporate realm, individuals often find themselves navigating through a maze of challenges and pressures. Recognizing the undeniable impact of stress on both personal well-being and organizational effectiveness, the adoption of effective stress reduction techniques has become a strategic imperative for modern businesses.

Mindfulness Practices: Encouraging mindfulness practices, such as meditation and deep breathing exercises, serves as a powerful antidote to the fast-paced nature of the corporate environment. These techniques promote present-moment awareness, reducing anxiety and enhancing mental clarity.

Stress Management Workshops: Instituting stress management workshops provides employees with valuable tools and strategies to identify, cope with, and mitigate stressors effectively. These programs foster a proactive approach to stress reduction, equipping individuals with practical skills.

Work-Life Balance Initiatives: Acknowledging the importance of maintaining a healthy work-life balance is fundamental. Organizations can promote this balance by setting realistic working hours, encouraging regular breaks, and discouraging a culture of excessive overtime.

Physical Exercise Programs: Integrating physical exercise programs into the workplace contributes not only to stress reduction but also to improve overall health. On-site fitness facilities, virtual workout sessions, or fitness challenges provide avenues for employees to prioritize their physical well-being.

Time Management Training: Offering training programs on effective time management empowers employees to navigate their workloads efficiently. By setting priorities, establishing realistic goals, and learning to manage time effectively, individuals can reduce the stress associated with overwhelming tasks.

Flexible Work Arrangements: Recognizing the diverse needs of employees, organizations can introduce flexible work arrangements. Remote work options, flexible schedules, or compressed workweeks allow individuals to better balance professional responsibilities with personal commitments.

Healthy Eating Initiatives: A well-nourished body contributes to better stress resilience. Organizations can promote healthy eating habits by providing nutritious snack options, educating employees on nutrition, and creating an environment that supports mindful eating.

Employee Assistance Programs (EAPs): Implementing Employee Assistance Programs (EAPs) demonstrates a commitment to supporting employees' mental health. Confidential counseling and support services within EAPs offer a resource for individuals to navigate personal or work-related stressors.

Social Connection Initiatives: Recognizing the importance of social connections in combating stress, organizations can encourage interactions among employees. Social initiatives, team-building activities, or communal spaces foster a supportive workplace community.

Clear Communication Practices: Establishing clear communication channels within the organization is crucial. Transparent communication helps reduce uncertainty and stress associated with organizational changes, promoting a culture of openness and trust.

By incorporating these stress reduction techniques, organizations can create a workplace environment that values and prioritizes the well-being of its workforce. The implementation of such strategies not only enhances the mental and physical health of employees but also contributes to a more resilient, engaged, and productive workforce. In the evolving landscape of the corporate world, these techniques serve as essential tools for navigating the complexities of professional life while fostering a culture of sustained well-being.

Practical exercises for Mindfulness and Stress Management

Mindful Breathing Breaks: Encourage employees to take short mindful breathing breaks throughout the day. Inhale deeply, hold for a few seconds, and exhale slowly. This practice helps reset the nervous system and promotes a sense of calm.

Daily Gratitude Journal: Introduce a daily gratitude journaling practice. Encourage employees to write down three things they are grateful for each day. This mindfulness exercise shifts focus to positive aspects, reducing stress and fostering a positive mindset.

Mindful Listening Meetings: Implement mindful listening exercises in meetings. Before discussions, allocate a few minutes for everyone to practice active listening without interruptions. This cultivates a focused and present mindset, enhancing communication and reducing stress.

Body Scan Meditation: Conduct guided body scan meditations during breaks. Employees can practice bringing attention to each part of their body, releasing tension and promoting relaxation. This technique enhances overall body awareness and reduces stress.

Mindful Walking Sessions: Encourage walking meetings or short mindful walking sessions. Employees can step outside, focus on their footsteps, and engage their senses. Physical movement combined with mindfulness contributes to stress reduction and increased clarity.

Stress-Reduction Workshops: Host workshops on stress reduction techniques. Invite experts to share strategies like progressive muscle relaxation, guided imagery, or mindfulness-based stress reduction. Providing tools empowers employees to manage stress effectively.

Mindful Technology Use: Promote mindful technology use by encouraging short breaks from screens. Apply the 20-20-20 rule: every 20 minutes, look at something 20 feet away for at least 20 seconds. This reduces eye strain and encourages a moment of mindfulness.

Desk Mindfulness Reminders: Distribute desk mindfulness prompts, such as small cards with mindful quotes or breathing exercises. These reminders serve as cues for employees to pause, breathe, and bring awareness to the present moment during busy workdays.

Mindfulness App Subscriptions: Provide subscriptions to mindfulness apps for employees. Apps like Headspace or Calm offer guided meditations, breathing exercises, and stress-relief programs that employees can access during breaks or after work.

Weekly Mindful Intentions: Set weekly mindful intentions as a team. Encourage employees to identify one aspect of their work or personal life on which they intend to focus mindfully. Sharing intentions fosters a supportive and mindful work culture.

Integrating these practical exercises and prompts into the business environment creates a foundation for mindfulness and stress management. As employees incorporate these practices into their routines, the workplace becomes a space where individuals can navigate challenges with greater resilience and well-being.

JULY: ETHICS AND INTEGRITY IN BUSINESS

The Stoic Code of Ethics

Stoicism, a philosophical school that emerged in ancient Greece, offers a profound and enduring code of ethics that continues to resonate in the modern world. Rooted in the teachings of thinkers like Zeno of Citium, Epictetus, and Seneca, the Stoic code of ethics provides a timeless guide to virtuous living, emphasizing principles that transcend cultural and temporal boundaries. At the core of Stoic ethics lies the concept of virtue, which the Stoics identified as the highest good. The four cardinal virtues—wisdom, courage, justice, and temperance—form the cornerstone of Stoic ethical philosophy. These virtues, considered intrinsic to human nature, serve as a compass for individuals navigating the complexities of life.

1. Wisdom (Sophia): Wisdom, in the Stoic context, extends beyond intellectual knowledge. It involves the practical application of reason to navigate life's challenges judiciously. Stoics believe in the pursuit of knowledge for the sake of virtuous living, emphasizing an understanding of the natural order of the world and the acceptance of what is beyond one's control.

2. Courage (Andreia): Courage, according to the Stoics, is the fortitude to face life's adversities with resilience. It is not merely physical bravery but the inner strength to endure hardships and maintain one's principles in the face of challenges. Stoicism encourages individuals to confront fears, practice self-discipline, and cultivate a steadfast resolve.

3. Justice (Dikaiosyne): Stoic justice revolves around treating others with fairness, kindness, and equity. It underscores the interconnectedness of humanity and the importance of contributing positively to the well-being of society. Stoics advocate for impartiality, empathy, and a commitment to upholding moral principles in interactions with others.

4. Temperance (Sophrosyne): Temperance, or self-control, involves mastering one's desires and impulses. Stoics believe in aligning personal desires with reason and adhering to a life of moderation. By practicing temperance, individuals avoid excessive attachments to material possessions or fleeting pleasures, fostering inner tranquility.

Central to Stoic ethics is the understanding that while external circumstances are beyond one's control, individuals possess the power to control their responses and attitudes. This principle, encapsulated in the Stoic concept of the dichotomy of control, emphasizes focusing energy on what can be influenced and accepting with equanimity what cannot. The Stoic code of ethics is not a rigid set of rules but a flexible guide that encourages individuals to continually strive for self-improvement and virtuous living. It promotes a mindset where individuals prioritize character over external circumstances, cultivate resilience in the face of challenges, and contribute positively to the welfare of the broader community.

In embracing the Stoic code of ethics, individuals find a profound framework for navigating the complexities of life with integrity, resilience, and a commitment to virtuous living—a timeless philosophy that transcends the boundaries of time and culture.

Navigating Ethical Dilemmas

Navigating ethical challenges in the business world requires a thoughtful and principled approach. Stoicism, a philosophical system rooted in ancient Greece, provides a timeless framework for businesses to address ethical dilemmas with clarity and virtue. In the corporate context, Stoicism encourages organizations to define and articulate their core values. Establishing a set of principles aligned with ethical business conduct—such as transparency, fairness, and social responsibility—forms the foundation for principled decision-making. The dichotomy of control, a fundamental Stoic concept, becomes directly applicable in business ethics. Leaders and employees are urged to focus on aspects within the company's control, fostering a proactive and principled approach to ethical decision-making despite external factors. Stoicism advocates for rational analysis in ethical decision-making within businesses. Corporate leaders are encouraged to objectively assess situations, consider potential consequences, and align choices with rational judgment. This approach promotes well-considered and ethically sound business decisions. Virtue, considered the highest good in Stoic philosophy, translates into the business context as the pursuit of ethical excellence. In corporate settings, decisions guided by wisdom, courage, justice, and temperance contribute to the establishment of a virtuous corporate culture.

Regular self-examination and reflection on corporate actions and decisions are integral to Stoic ethics. Businesses are encouraged to engage in introspection, ensuring that their choices align with their defined values and contribute to the ethical development of the corporate identity. While perfection may be unattainable, Stoicism's ideal of the sage serves as an inspiration for ethical business leadership. Executives and managers can strive for moral excellence, setting an example for the organization and fostering a culture of ethical decision-making. Stoicism instills resilience in businesses by teaching them to accept the consequences of their ethical choices, even when external outcomes are beyond their control. This resilience is crucial for maintaining ethical standards in the face of potential challenges or criticisms. Compassion and justice are emphasized in Stoic ethics as integral components of decision-making. Corporations are urged to consider the well-being of stakeholders, strive for fairness in dealings, and contribute to the broader societal good, aligning business operations with ethical principles.

In summary, Stoicism serves as a pragmatic guide for ethical decision-making in the corporate arena. By defining core values, applying the dichotomy of control, employing rational decision-making processes, prioritizing virtue, engaging in self-examination, aspiring toward Stoic leadership ideals, cultivating resilience, and embodying compassion and justice, businesses can navigate ethical dilemmas with moral clarity and contribute to a culture of integrity and ethical excellence. Stoicism thus becomes a cornerstone for fostering ethical business practices and upholding corporate responsibility in a complex and dynamic commercial landscape.

Building a Business with Integrity

Building a business with integrity is a noble and challenging endeavor that requires a steadfast commitment to ethical principles, transparency, and a genuine concern for the well-being of stakeholders. In navigating the complexities of the corporate landscape, a Stoic-inspired approach provides a profound framework for entrepreneurs and business leaders to forge a path marked by virtue, honesty, and long-term success.

Defining Core Values: At the heart of building a business with integrity lies the definition and unwavering adherence to core values. Stoicism encourages entrepreneurs to identify and articulate values that reflect ethical business conduct. These values serve as the guiding principles that shape every aspect of the business, from decision-making to customer interactions.

Embodying Ethical Leadership: Integrity begins at the top, and ethical leadership is paramount in building a business with a strong moral foundation. Entrepreneurs should strive to embody Stoic ideals of wisdom, courage, justice, and temperance in their leadership style. This includes making decisions that prioritize long-term ethical considerations over short-term gains and fostering a culture of trust and accountability.

Transparency in Operations: Stoicism emphasizes rationality and honesty in all endeavors. In the business context, this translates to a commitment to transparency in operations. Building a business with integrity requires open communication with stakeholders, including customers, employees, and investors. Transparent business practices build trust and credibility, essential elements for long-term success.

Ethical Decision-Making: Stoic philosophy encourages rational analysis and the consideration of consequences in decision-making. Entrepreneurs building a business with integrity should approach dilemmas with a focus on ethical considerations. This involves weighing the impact of decisions on all stakeholders, avoiding shortcuts that compromise integrity, and making choices aligned with the core values of the business.

Prioritizing Customer Satisfaction: A business built with integrity places a high premium on customer satisfaction. Stoicism emphasizes the importance of justice in all dealings, and in a business context, this means providing products or services that meet or exceed customer expectations. Ethical entrepreneurs prioritize customer well-being, ensuring fair treatment and honest representation of their offerings.

Stewardship of Resources: Stoicism encourages the wise and moderate use of resources. In building a business with integrity, entrepreneurs should adopt sustainable and responsible practices. This involves considering the environmental and social impact of business operations, embracing corporate social responsibility, and contributing positively to the community.

Empathy and Employee Well-being: Building a business with integrity extends to the well-being of employees. Stoic principles underscore the importance of compassion, and this applies to the treatment of the workforce. Ethical entrepreneurs cultivate a workplace culture that values the health, safety, and personal development of employees, fostering loyalty and commitment.

Long-Term Vision over Short-Term Gain: Stoicism advocates for a focus on the long-term rather than succumbing to immediate gratification. In the business context, this means resisting the temptation of unethical shortcuts for short-term gains. Entrepreneurs with integrity prioritize the sustained success of the business, understanding that ethical practices contribute to long-term profitability and reputation.

Acceptance of Responsibility: Stoicism teaches the acceptance of responsibility for one's actions. In building a business with integrity, entrepreneurs acknowledge mistakes, learn from them, and take proactive measures to rectify any harm caused. Accepting responsibility fosters a culture of accountability and resilience in the face of challenges.

Contributing to the Greater Good: Finally, building a business with integrity involves a commitment to contributing to the greater good. Stoicism encourages entrepreneurs to recognize their role in the broader community and society. Ethical businesses actively seek opportunities to make positive contributions, whether through philanthropy, ethical sourcing practices, or community engagement.

In conclusion, building a business with integrity requires a comprehensive and principled approach inspired by Stoic philosophy. By defining core values, embodying ethical leadership, prioritizing transparency, making ethical decisions, focusing on customer satisfaction, stewarding resources responsibly, prioritizing employee well-being, emphasizing a long-term vision, accepting responsibility, and contributing to the greater good, entrepreneurs can establish businesses that stand the test of time and contribute positively to the world. Stoicism provides a timeless guide for entrepreneurs who aspire to build not just successful enterprises but ones that are deeply rooted in integrity and ethical principles.

Practical exercises for Ethics and Integrity in business

Values Clarification Workshop: Conduct a workshop with employees to collectively identify and clarify the core values that should guide the business. Encourage open discussion to ensure alignment and understanding of these values, fostering a shared commitment to ethical conduct.

Stoic Decision-Making Scenarios: Develop hypothetical scenarios based on real-world ethical challenges. Encourage employees to apply Stoic principles, such as the dichotomy of control and rational analysis, to navigate these scenarios and make decisions that uphold integrity.

Transparency Training Session: Organize a training session on the importance of transparency in business operations. Provide practical examples of how transparency builds trust and offer guidelines for communicating openly with stakeholders, both internally and externally.

Customer Impact Assessment: Before implementing changes or launching new products/services, conduct a customer impact assessment. Evaluate potential consequences on customers, ensuring that business decisions prioritize their satisfaction and well-being, in line with Stoic principles of justice.

Ethical Leadership Reflections: Encourage leaders to engage in regular reflections on their leadership practices. Prompt them to consider how their decisions align with Stoic virtues and whether their actions contribute to building a culture of integrity within the organization.

Employee Code of Ethics Workshop: Collaborate with employees to co-create a code of ethics specific to the organization. This workshop can involve brainstorming sessions to gather input and perspectives, fostering a sense of ownership and commitment to ethical guidelines.

Sustainability Impact Assessment: Develop a sustainability impact assessment tool to evaluate the environmental and social consequences of business activities. This exercise encourages businesses to adopt responsible and sustainable practices, aligning with Stoic principles of responsible resource stewardship.

Integrity Checkpoints in Projects: Integrate integrity checkpoints into project management processes. At key milestones, assess whether the project aligns with ethical guidelines, ensuring that short-term goals do not compromise long-term integrity and reputation.

Empathy Training for Customer-Facing Roles: Provide empathy training for employees in customer-facing roles. Using real-world scenarios, this exercise helps employees understand and practice empathy, a Stoic principle that fosters compassionate and just interactions with customers.

Community Engagement Initiatives: Develop initiatives that actively engage the business with the local community. This can include volunteering programs, partnerships with local organizations, or ethical sourcing practices. Such initiatives align with Stoic principles of contributing to the greater good.

These practical exercises and prompts are designed to instill ethical behavior and integrity within a business, drawing inspiration from Stoic philosophy. By integrating these activities into the organizational culture, businesses can nurture a commitment to ethical conduct among employees, ultimately fostering a workplace environment rooted in integrity and virtue.

AUGUST: COLLABORATION AND TEAMWORK

The Power of Collaboration

Collaboration in the business world isn't merely a catchphrase; it's a dynamic force that propels innovation, fosters problem-solving, and steers companies toward sustainable growth. This collaborative spirit transcends traditional teamwork, embracing a collective approach that draws inspiration from diverse perspectives. Businesses tapping into the power of collaboration unlock new opportunities, cultivate creativity, and navigate the complexities of the modern marketplace. Diversity lies at the heart of collaborative innovation. When individuals with varied backgrounds, experiences, and expertise come together, the collision of diverse perspectives sparks creativity. This convergence often leads to groundbreaking ideas that can revolutionize products, services, and business processes. A real-world example is the story of a tech company where developers, designers, and marketing professionals collaborated closely, leveraging their diverse skills to launch an innovative app that gained widespread acclaim. Breaking down silos is another aspect of collaboration's impact. In organizations where departments operate in isolation, collaboration becomes the key to facilitating cross-functional communication. This collaborative approach fosters efficiency and effectiveness, enabling businesses to develop comprehensive solutions that address multifaceted challenges.

Collaboration enhances problem-solving agility, a critical advantage in the ever-changing business landscape. Teams that work together, pooling their collective intelligence and skills, become more adept at identifying solutions and adapting to evolving circumstances. This agility becomes a significant competitive edge in dynamic markets. A culture of knowledge sharing and continuous learning emerges naturally in collaborative environments. When employees collaborate, they exchange ideas, insights, and best practices, fostering a culture of curiosity and learning. This culture positions businesses as hubs of intellectual growth and sets them apart as industry leaders. Cross-functional collaboration is crucial for the success of various projects. Many initiatives require input from different departments and skill sets. Collaboration ensures that projects benefit from a well-rounded set of skills and expertise, enhancing the likelihood of success. Collaborating closely with clients is another facet of collaboration's impact. Businesses that involve clients in the collaborative process, understanding their needs and goals, can tailor solutions more effectively. This collaborative client approach fosters stronger partnerships, customer satisfaction, and loyalty. The agile response to market changes is a direct result of collaboration. In fast-paced markets, the ability to respond swiftly to changes is critical. Collaborative organizations are better positioned to adapt to market shifts by involving various stakeholders in decision-making processes, gathering real-time insights, and adjusting strategies with agility.

Collaboration contributes to the creation of a positive and inclusive work environment. When employees feel their contributions are valued and have opportunities to collaborate, it enhances morale and job satisfaction. This positive atmosphere, in turn, attracts and retains top talent, creating a virtuous cycle of productivity and innovation. It's important to note that collaboration also fosters collective responsibility and accountability. Teams working together toward common goals create a sense of shared commitment to success. This shared responsibility enhances accountability as team members understand the impact of their contributions on the overall outcome. In the face of remote work challenges, collaboration has proven to be a valuable asset. Businesses that invest in effective collaboration platforms and foster a collaborative mindset are better equipped to overcome the challenges of remote work, ensuring continuity and productivity.

In essence, the power of collaboration isn't just a business strategy; it's a transformative force that nurtures innovation, adapts to change, and builds resilient organizations. Businesses that harness this power create a culture of creativity, inclusivity, and continuous improvement, positioning themselves for sustained success in an ever-evolving market. Collaborative initiatives aren't just about working together; they're about unlocking the collective potential that propels organizations toward a future of growth and prosperity.

Cultivating a Positive Team Culture

Cultivating a positive team culture is not merely an aspiration but a strategic imperative that significantly influences organizational success. A positive team culture fosters collaboration, enhances productivity, and creates a work environment where individuals thrive. Beyond the surface level, it's about establishing a collective mindset that values each team member's contribution and creates a shared commitment to success. At the heart of cultivating a positive team culture is the emphasis on open communication and mutual respect. When team members feel comfortable expressing their thoughts, ideas, concerns, and feedback, it creates an atmosphere of trust. This open dialogue fosters a sense of belonging and ensures that everyone's voice is heard, contributing to a positive and inclusive work environment. Recognition and appreciation are essential components of a positive team culture. Acknowledging and celebrating individual and collective achievements boosts morale and reinforces a sense of accomplishment. Whether it's a small accomplishment or a significant milestone, recognizing efforts fosters a culture where team members feel valued and motivated to contribute their best. Leaders play a pivotal role in shaping team culture. Leaders who lead by example, demonstrating integrity, empathy, and a commitment to the team's well-being, set the tone for a positive culture. When leaders prioritize transparency, actively listen to team members, and show genuine care for their development, it creates a positive leadership model that permeates the entire team.

Collaboration is the lifeblood of a positive team culture. Encouraging teamwork and breaking down silos foster a collective approach to problem-solving and goal achievement. Teams that collaborate effectively leverage diverse skills and perspectives, creating a dynamic environment where innovation thrives. A positive team culture is closely tied to a growth mindset. Cultivating an environment that encourages continuous learning and embraces challenges as opportunities for growth fosters resilience and adaptability. Team members are more likely to take on challenges and view setbacks as learning experiences when a growth mindset is ingrained in the team culture. Trust is the foundation upon which positive team cultures are built. Team members must trust each other and their leaders to collaborate effectively. Building trust involves consistency, reliability, and a commitment to delivering on promises. Trustworthy teams operate with transparency and integrity, reinforcing a positive and cohesive culture. Flexibility is a key element of a positive team culture, especially in today's dynamic work landscape. Teams that can adapt to change and embrace flexibility in work arrangements create an environment where individuals feel supported and empowered to navigate the evolving challenges of their roles. Empathy is a cornerstone of positive team culture. Understanding and appreciating the unique strengths, challenges, and perspectives of each team member creates a supportive and compassionate work environment. Teams that prioritize empathy are better equipped to handle conflicts, foster collaboration, and promote overall well-being. Celebrating diversity and inclusion is integral to a positive team culture. Embracing a diverse range of backgrounds, experiences, and ideas enriches team dynamics. Inclusive teams leverage the strengths that diversity brings, creating an environment where creativity and innovation thrive.

Lastly, a positive team culture is sustained through a commitment to well-being. Encouraging work-life balance, providing resources for mental health, and prioritizing the holistic well-being of team members contribute to a positive and sustainable work culture. A real-world example that illustrates the impact of a positive team culture is the story of a software development team. The team, led by a supportive and empathetic manager, created a culture of open communication, collaboration, and continuous learning. Team members felt valued and recognized for their contributions, leading to a high level of job satisfaction and innovation. The positive team culture not only enhanced productivity but also contributed to the retention of top talent and the overall success of the projects undertaken by the team.

In conclusion, cultivating a positive team culture is a multifaceted endeavor that requires intentional efforts from both leaders and team members. It goes beyond superficial gestures and involves fostering a mindset that values collaboration, continuous learning, trust, and empathy. Organizations that invest in cultivating a positive team culture not only create a conducive work environment but also position themselves for sustained success in the ever-evolving landscape of the professional world.

Resolving Conflict with Stoic Principles

Resolving conflicts is an inevitable aspect of professional life, and approaching them with Stoic principles can provide a thoughtful and effective framework for resolution. Stoicism, an ancient philosophy originating in Greece, offers timeless wisdom that encourages individuals to navigate conflicts with reason, self-control, and a commitment to virtue. Applying Stoic principles to conflict resolution fosters a mindset that prioritizes understanding, empathy, and constructive dialogue. At the core of Stoic conflict resolution is the principle of maintaining equanimity in the face of adversity. When conflicts arise, individuals are encouraged to embrace the Stoic concept of the "dichotomy of control." This means focusing on what can be controlled – one's own reactions, emotions, and choices – and accepting what cannot be controlled, such as the actions and perspectives of others. By internalizing this principle, individuals gain a sense of empowerment and composure, enabling them to approach conflicts with a calm and rational mindset. Stoicism emphasizes the importance of rational analysis in conflict resolution. When faced with a disagreement or dispute, individuals are encouraged to step back and objectively assess the situation. This involves examining the facts, considering different perspectives, and identifying the underlying causes of the conflict. By applying rational analysis, individuals can move beyond emotional reactions and work toward a clearer understanding of the issues at hand. The Stoic commitment to virtue plays a pivotal role in conflict resolution. Virtues such as wisdom, courage, justice, and temperance guide individuals in their responses to conflicts. Wisdom encourages thoughtful consideration of the consequences of actions, while courage fosters the strength to address conflicts directly. Justice emphasizes fairness and a commitment to finding equitable solutions, and temperance promotes moderation in responses, avoiding impulsive reactions.

Empathy is another Stoic principle that proves invaluable in resolving conflicts. Stoicism encourages individuals to cultivate an understanding of others' perspectives and motivations. By empathizing with the experiences and concerns of those involved in the conflict, individuals can foster a more compassionate and cooperative approach to resolution. This aligns with the Stoic belief in the interconnectedness of humanity and the importance of treating others with kindness and understanding. Stoicism underscores the significance of accepting responsibility for one's actions. In conflict resolution, this involves acknowledging one's role in the disagreement and taking accountability for any mistakes or miscommunications. By doing so, individuals demonstrate integrity and contribute to the creation of a constructive resolution process. A practical example illustrating the application of Stoic principles in conflict resolution is a scenario involving two team members in a project. The conflict arises from differing opinions on the project's direction. Applying Stoic principles, both individuals first focus on understanding their own reactions and emotions, recognizing what is within their control. They then engage in rational analysis, objectively assessing the facts and perspectives involved. Drawing on the virtues of courage and justice, they address the conflict directly, expressing their viewpoints with clarity and fairness. Empathy comes into play as they actively listen to each other's concerns, seeking to understand the motivations and experiences influencing their perspectives. Accepting responsibility, they acknowledge any misunderstandings and mistakes, contributing to a collaborative atmosphere. The Stoic approach to conflict resolution enables them to navigate the disagreement with composure, reason, and a commitment to virtuous conduct, ultimately finding a solution that aligns with the project's goals.

In conclusion, resolving conflicts with Stoic principles offers a holistic and principled approach. By embracing the dichotomy of control, rational analysis, virtues, empathy, and responsibility, individuals can navigate conflicts with composure and foster solutions that align with ethical principles. Stoicism provides a timeless guide for conflict resolution that transcends situational dynamics, contributing to a workplace culture characterized by understanding, cooperation, and integrity.

Practical exercises for Collaboration and Teamwork

Values Alignment Workshop: Conduct a workshop to identify and articulate the core values that guide the business. Encourage team members to discuss and align individual values with the organizational values. This exercise fosters a shared understanding of the principles that guide collaborative efforts.

Cross-Functional Problem-Solving Sessions: Organize regular problem-solving sessions that involve team members from different departments. Present a real or hypothetical challenge, and encourage diverse perspectives to find comprehensive solutions. This exercise promotes collaboration across functional boundaries.

Team-Building Retreat: Plan a team-building retreat that includes activities designed to promote trust, communication, and camaraderie. Engaging in non-work-related activities in a relaxed setting helps team members build personal connections, fostering a collaborative atmosphere.

Rotational Task Assignments: Implement a system of rotational task assignments where team members take on roles outside their usual responsibilities. This exposes individuals to different aspects of the business and encourages a more holistic understanding, fostering collaboration through shared knowledge.

Collaborative Goal Setting: Instead of top-down goal-setting, involve the entire team in the process. Facilitate a collaborative goal-setting session where team members contribute their perspectives, ensuring that everyone feels a sense of ownership and commitment to the shared objectives.

Peer Recognition Program: Establish a peer recognition program where team members acknowledge and appreciate each other's contributions. This exercise not only boosts morale but also reinforces the idea that collaboration and teamwork are valued within the organization.

Role-Playing Communication Scenarios: Develop communication scenarios relevant to business interactions and have team members role-play these situations. This exercise enhances communication skills, empathy, and understanding, contributing to more effective collaboration in real-world scenarios.

Diversity and Inclusion Workshops: Conduct workshops focused on diversity and inclusion. Help team members understand the importance of diverse perspectives and create an inclusive environment. This fosters collaboration by celebrating differences and leveraging a broad range of experiences.

Team Learning Circles: Establish learning circles within the team where members take turns sharing insights, industry updates, or relevant articles. This knowledge-sharing exercise promotes continuous learning and creates a culture of collaboration built on a foundation of shared knowledge.

Reflection and Improvement Sessions: Regularly schedule reflection sessions where the team evaluates past projects, discusses successes and challenges, and collaboratively identifies areas for improvement. This exercise not only enhances team collaboration but also contributes to a culture of continuous improvement.

These practical exercises and prompts are designed to actively engage team members, foster collaboration, and strengthen the overall teamwork within a business. By incorporating these activities into the regular workflow, businesses can nurture a collaborative culture that contributes to innovation, efficiency, and a positive working environment.

SEPTEMBER: ENTREPRENEURIAL MINDSET

Cultivating an Entrepreneurial Spirit

Cultivating an entrepreneurial spirit within an organization is a dynamic and transformative journey that goes beyond traditional business practices. It involves fostering a mindset that embraces innovation, risk-taking, and a proactive approach to challenges. In the rapidly evolving landscape of the business world, instilling an entrepreneurial spirit is crucial for organizations to adapt, thrive, and drive meaningful change. At the core of cultivating an entrepreneurial spirit is the encouragement of creative thinking. Entrepreneurs are known for their ability to think outside the box, and organizations can foster this mindset by creating an environment that values and rewards innovation. Establishing innovation hubs, encouraging brainstorming sessions, and providing dedicated time for creative exploration are practical ways to stimulate and nurture creative thinking within a team. Risk-taking is a fundamental element of entrepreneurship. Cultivating an entrepreneurial spirit involves encouraging calculated risk-taking within the organization. This doesn't mean recklessness; rather, it involves creating a culture where individuals feel empowered to propose and implement new ideas, even if they come with a degree of uncertainty. Celebrating and learning from both successes and failures contributes to a culture that views risk as an inherent part of growth.

An entrepreneurial spirit thrives on a sense of ownership and accountability. Leaders can empower team members by giving them autonomy and responsibility for their projects. When individuals feel a strong sense of ownership, they are more likely to approach challenges with an entrepreneurial mindset, taking initiative and driving projects forward with a sense of personal commitment. Continuous learning is a hallmark of entrepreneurial success. Organizations can foster an entrepreneurial spirit by promoting a culture of ongoing education and skill development. Providing resources for training, encouraging participation in industry events, and supporting educational opportunities contribute to a workforce that is constantly evolving and adapting to change. Entrepreneurs are known for their agility and ability to pivot in response to market changes. Organizations can instill this adaptive mindset by promoting a culture of flexibility. This involves being open to change, encouraging employees to embrace new approaches, and fostering an environment where adjustments can be made swiftly in response to emerging opportunities or challenges. Collaboration is a key component of entrepreneurial success. Cultivating an entrepreneurial spirit involves breaking down silos within the organization and promoting cross-functional collaboration. Encouraging diverse teams to work together fosters the exchange of ideas and perspectives, fueling innovation and problem-solving.

An entrepreneurial spirit is closely tied to a customer-centric approach. Organizations can cultivate this mindset by placing a strong emphasis on understanding customer needs and preferences. Regular customer feedback, market research, and a commitment to delivering value contribute to an entrepreneurial culture that is responsive to the demands of the market. Leadership plays a pivotal role in fostering an entrepreneurial spirit. Leaders who embody entrepreneurial qualities, such as vision, resilience, and a willingness to take calculated risks, serve as role models for the rest of the organization. Leadership that encourages and supports entrepreneurial initiatives sets the tone for a culture that values innovation and proactive problem-solving. Encouraging intrapreneurship, or entrepreneurial activities within the confines of the organization, is an effective strategy for cultivating an entrepreneurial spirit. Providing opportunities for employees to propose and implement their own projects, experiment with new ideas, and potentially develop new products or services creates an environment where entrepreneurial thinking is not only encouraged but rewarded. Recognizing and celebrating entrepreneurial achievements is a crucial aspect of fostering an entrepreneurial spirit. Establishing awards, acknowledgment programs, or innovation showcases creates a culture that values and reinforces the entrepreneurial mindset. This recognition not only motivates individuals but also communicates to the entire organization that entrepreneurial contributions are highly valued.

In conclusion, cultivating an entrepreneurial spirit within an organization is a multifaceted and ongoing effort that involves nurturing a mindset of creativity, risk-taking, ownership, continuous learning, flexibility, collaboration, customer-centricity, and leadership. By actively promoting these qualities and creating an environment that supports entrepreneurial initiatives, organizations can position themselves to adapt, innovate, and thrive in the face of ever-changing business dynamics. The entrepreneurial spirit becomes a driving force for growth, resilience, and sustained success in today's dynamic business landscape.

Embracing Risk and Failure

Embracing risk and failure is a fundamental aspect of fostering innovation, growth, and resilience within the business landscape. In a world where uncertainty is inevitable, organizations that cultivate a culture of embracing risk and viewing failure as a stepping stone to success are better positioned to adapt, learn, and ultimately thrive. Taking risks is synonymous with entrepreneurship, and organizations looking to instill a culture of innovation must encourage their teams to step outside their comfort zones. This involves creating an environment where calculated risks are not only accepted but celebrated. Leaders play a pivotal role in this process by setting an example, demonstrating a willingness to take risks themselves, and fostering a culture that views risk as an essential part of progress. A crucial element in embracing risk is creating a safe space for experimentation and learning. Encouraging employees to test new ideas, even if they come with the possibility of failure, promotes a mindset of continuous improvement. Establishing innovation labs, pilot projects, or dedicated spaces for experimentation allows teams to explore uncharted territories without the fear of immediate consequences. Failure, far from being a setback, should be reframed as a valuable learning experience. Organizations that embrace failure as a natural part of the innovation process create an atmosphere where individuals feel empowered to take risks without the paralyzing fear of reprisal. Learning from failure becomes a catalyst for improvement and innovation rather than a cause for punishment.

One effective strategy for embracing failure is conducting post-mortem analyses. When a project doesn't meet its objectives, teams can gather to assess what went wrong, what could have been done differently, and what valuable insights can be gleaned from the experience. This process not only encourages transparency but also transforms failure into a constructive learning opportunity. Innovation often arises from the willingness to challenge the status quo, and that inherently involves an element of risk. Organizations that encourage a culture of questioning and curiosity foster an entrepreneurial mindset. Team members who feel empowered to ask "what if" and challenge existing norms contribute to an environment where risk-taking becomes ingrained in the organizational DNA. An illustrative example of embracing risk and failure is found in the story of a tech startup. The company encouraged its development team to experiment with a cutting-edge technology in a new product. While the initial launch didn't meet expectations and could be perceived as a failure, the organization viewed it as a valuable learning experience. The team conducted a thorough analysis, identified areas for improvement, and used the insights gained to pivot successfully in the next iteration, ultimately creating a groundbreaking product.

In conclusion, embracing risk and failure is not merely a business strategy; it's a cultural shift that positions organizations for resilience and success in an ever-changing environment. By fostering a mindset that values experimentation, learns from setbacks, and views risk as an integral part of progress, businesses create a foundation for innovation and continuous improvement. Through calculated risk-taking and the lessons gleaned from failure, organizations can navigate uncertainty, adapt to change, and ultimately emerge stronger in the face of evolving challenges.

Persisting in the Face of Challenges

In the dynamic landscape of business, persisting in the face of challenges is not just a desirable trait; it's a survival skill that distinguishes those who thrive from those who falter. Consider the story of a manufacturing company that faced a significant downturn in the market due to unforeseen economic challenges. Instead of succumbing to the immediate pressure and accepting defeat, the leadership team recognized the importance of persistence. Faced with declining revenues and increased competition, the company could have opted for a reactive approach, cutting costs indiscriminately and retreating from innovation. However, the leadership team chose a different path. They gathered the entire organization to communicate transparently about the challenges ahead and the need for collective perseverance. Rather than viewing the downturn as an insurmountable obstacle, the leadership team saw it as an opportunity to reinvent the business. They initiated a comprehensive analysis of market trends, customer needs, and internal capabilities. This proactive approach led to the identification of new product opportunities and untapped markets, laying the groundwork for a strategic pivot. The company implemented cost-saving measures judiciously, aligning them with the overarching goal of innovation and market expansion. Instead of laying off employees, they invested in training programs to enhance skills and adapt to the evolving market demands. This commitment to the growth and development of their workforce created a sense of shared purpose and determination.

In addition to internal initiatives, the leadership actively sought input from employees at all levels. Recognizing that innovative solutions could emerge from any corner of the organization, they fostered an environment where every team member felt empowered to contribute ideas. This inclusive approach not only generated fresh perspectives but also instilled a collective commitment to overcoming challenges. Through persistent efforts and a commitment to staying true to their core values, the company weathered the storm. The strategic pivot, fueled by innovation and resilience, not only allowed them to survive the downturn but positioned them as a more agile and competitive player in the market. The challenges they faced became catalysts for positive change, demonstrating that with persistence, a company can emerge stronger and more adaptable than ever before. This real-world example highlights the transformative power of persistence in the business realm. It underscores the importance of maintaining a clear vision, adopting proactive problem-solving approaches, cultivating a growth mindset, and learning from setbacks. Organizations that embrace these principles not only navigate challenges successfully but also create a culture where persistence is not just a response to adversity but a driving force behind sustained growth and success.

Practical exercises for Entrepreneurial Mindset

Vision Board Workshop: Have team members create individual or collaborative vision boards that depict their entrepreneurial aspirations. Encourage them to include personal and professional goals, innovative ideas, and the impact they want to make. This exercise helps visualize and solidify entrepreneurial ambitions.

Failure Resilience Journaling: Provide team members with journals to reflect on past failures, reframing them as valuable learning experiences. Encourage them to identify lessons learned, skills acquired, and how those setbacks contributed to their entrepreneurial journey. This exercise fosters resilience and a positive attitude toward failure.

Opportunity Recognition Game: Conduct a game where participants identify potential business opportunities in everyday scenarios. This prompts them to think creatively and enhances their ability to recognize possibilities, a key trait of an entrepreneurial mindset.

Innovation Sprint: Organize a time-limited brainstorming session focused on generating innovative ideas for a specific challenge or opportunity. Set a strict time constraint to simulate the fast-paced decision-making required in entrepreneurial settings. This exercise encourages quick thinking and adaptability.

Pitch Perfect Workshop: Equip team members with the skills to pitch their ideas effectively. Provide training on crafting compelling elevator pitches and conduct mock pitch sessions. This exercise hones communication skills and prepares individuals to present ideas with confidence, a vital aspect of the entrepreneurial mindset.

Networking Challenge: Task team members with expanding their professional network by connecting with a predetermined number of individuals within a specified time frame. This exercise promotes proactive relationship-building, a characteristic of successful entrepreneurs.

Resource Scarcity Simulation: Create a scenario where resources are limited, forcing team members to strategize and innovate within constraints. This exercise simulates the resource challenges often faced by entrepreneurs, fostering adaptability and creative problem-solving.

Entrepreneurial Book Club: Initiate a book club focused on entrepreneurial literature. Select books that inspire innovation, resilience, and an entrepreneurial mindset. Encourage discussions about how the concepts from the books can be applied in the team's day-to-day work.

SWOT Analysis of Personal Skills: Have team members conduct a personal SWOT (Strengths, Weaknesses, Opportunities, and Threats) analysis of their skills and abilities. This exercise helps individuals identify areas for improvement and areas where they can leverage their strengths in entrepreneurial endeavors.

Mock Business Plan Competition: Organize a friendly competition where team members create and present mock business plans for innovative ideas. This exercise not only allows them to apply entrepreneurial thinking but also fosters a sense of healthy competition and camaraderie.

These practical exercises and prompts are designed to immerse individuals in the entrepreneurial mindset, fostering creativity, resilience, adaptability, and a proactive approach to challenges. By integrating these

106

activities into the team's routine, organizations can cultivate an entrepreneurial culture that propels innovation and success.

OCTOBER: REFLECTION AND GRATITUDE

Daily Reflection Practices

In the realm of business, daily reflection practices are invaluable for professionals seeking continuous improvement, strategic clarity, and enhanced performance. These reflective exercises not only contribute to personal development but also align individual efforts with organizational goals. Here's how daily reflection practices can be tailored to a business context:

Project Review Journal: Start or end the day by journaling about the day's work on ongoing projects. Reflecting on progress, challenges faced, and potential solutions provides clarity and insight. This practice ensures that individuals stay focused on project objectives and adapt as needed.

Gratitude in the Workplace: Integrate gratitude exercises into the daily routine at work. Reflecting on positive aspects of the work environment, collaborative efforts, or achievements fosters a positive workplace culture. This practice enhances team morale and resilience.

Strategic Goal Alignment Sessions: Dedicate time daily to reflect on progress toward strategic organizational goals. Individuals can assess how their daily activities contribute to overarching objectives. This reflective exercise ensures that actions align with the broader business strategy.

Mindful Decision-Making: Before key meetings or decision points, engage in short mindfulness sessions. Mindful practices enhance focus, reduce stress, and improve decision-making. This reflective exercise is particularly beneficial in fast-paced business environments.

SWOT Analysis for Professional Growth: Regularly conduct a personal SWOT analysis focusing on professional skills and capabilities. Reflecting on strengths, weaknesses, opportunities, and threats supports intentional professional development. This practice is vital for staying adaptable in a competitive business landscape.

Client Feedback Reflection: Reflect on client feedback received throughout the day. Whether positive or constructive, analyzing client responses enhances service quality and client relationships. This reflective exercise contributes to continuous improvement and client satisfaction.

Learning Log for Skill Enhancement: Keep a learning log to record new industry insights, skills acquired, or lessons learned each day. Reflecting on daily learnings ensures professionals stay abreast of industry trends and continuously enhance their skill set to remain competitive.

Recognition of Team Achievements: Acknowledge and reflect on the daily achievements of team members. Celebrating small wins fosters a positive team culture and reinforces a sense of collective accomplishment. This reflective practice contributes to team motivation and cohesion.

Emotional Intelligence Check-In: Take moments throughout the day to reflect on emotional responses in professional interactions. Recognizing and understanding emotions enhances emotional intelligence, facilitating more effective communication and collaboration.

Time Management Audit Reflection: Reflect on how time was allocated during the workday. This exercise promotes awareness of time management and ensures that time is spent on tasks that align with organizational priorities. It encourages intentional use of time for maximum business impact.

Incorporating these business-related daily reflection practices empowers professionals to navigate their workdays with intention, contributing to individual and organizational success. The reflective mindset cultivated through these practices supports strategic thinking, adaptability, and a proactive approach to achieving business objectives.

Cultivating Gratitude in Business

Cultivating gratitude in the business environment is a powerful practice that goes beyond mere politeness; it contributes to a positive workplace culture, enhances team dynamics, and fosters overall organizational well-being. Gratitude, when integrated into the fabric of a business, becomes a catalyst for increased employee engagement, improved collaboration, and a resilient team spirit. Expressing gratitude in the workplace can take various forms, and it begins with leadership setting the tone. Leaders who openly acknowledge and appreciate the efforts of their team members create a culture where gratitude is not just encouraged but expected. This acknowledgment can be conveyed through regular team meetings, personalized messages, or public recognition, demonstrating the value placed on individual contributions. Encouraging employees to express gratitude towards one another establishes a reciprocal atmosphere of appreciation. Implementing a peer recognition program or providing platforms for team members to acknowledge each other's efforts fosters a sense of camaraderie. This practice enhances team cohesion and reinforces a positive feedback loop within the organization.

Gratitude can also be integrated into organizational rituals and routines. For example, starting or ending meetings with a brief gratitude round where team members express appreciation for a colleague's support or a project milestone creates a positive and uplifting atmosphere. This simple yet impactful practice contributes to a culture of mutual respect and acknowledgment. Incorporating gratitude into employee development programs can further enhance professional relationships. Encouraging mentorship and recognizing the guidance provided by experienced team members instills a sense of gratitude for knowledge-sharing and skill development. This practice not only facilitates knowledge transfer but also strengthens the collaborative fabric of the organization. The benefits of cultivating gratitude extend to client relationships as well. Expressing gratitude towards clients for their trust, collaboration, and feedback builds a foundation of goodwill. This appreciation contributes to client loyalty, fosters long-term partnerships, and enhances the reputation of the business in the market. An organization that actively cultivates gratitude is better equipped to navigate challenges with resilience. When facing difficulties, expressing gratitude for the collective effort and acknowledging the team's commitment reinforces a sense of purpose. This positive outlook contributes to a solutions-oriented mindset, encouraging the team to tackle challenges with determination and unity. One notable example of gratitude in business is seen in a tech startup that, during a challenging period, expressed gratitude towards its employees for their dedication and adaptability. The leadership team organized a gratitude-themed event, highlighting individual achievements and team milestones. This practice not only boosted morale but also created a more positive and resilient work environment, ultimately contributing to the company's ability to overcome challenges.

In conclusion, cultivating gratitude in business is not just a nicety but a strategic practice that significantly impacts organizational culture and performance. From leadership acknowledgment to peer recognition, and from integrating gratitude into routines to expressing appreciation to clients, fostering a culture of gratitude contributes to a workplace where individuals feel valued, motivated, and empowered to bring their best selves to their professional roles. This intentional cultivation of gratitude becomes a driving force for positive organizational dynamics and sustained success.

Celebrating Successes, Big and Small

Celebrating successes, whether monumental achievements or small victories, is a crucial component of fostering a positive and dynamic workplace culture. Recognizing and commemorating accomplishments not only boosts morale but also reinforces a culture of appreciation, motivation, and collective achievement. From significant milestones to everyday wins, celebrating successes creates a positive feedback loop that contributes to increased engagement and sustained team motivation. One of the key aspects of celebrating successes is the impact it has on employee morale. Recognizing and acknowledging individual and team accomplishments validates the hard work and dedication that employees invest in their roles. This validation not only boosts confidence but also creates a sense of fulfillment and purpose, fostering a positive and supportive work environment. The celebration of successes, big and small, contributes to the formation of a cohesive team. When individuals feel that their contributions are valued and recognized, it strengthens the sense of camaraderie within the team. This positive interpersonal dynamic enhances collaboration, communication, and the overall synergy needed for collective success. Leaders play a pivotal role in setting the tone for celebrating successes. When leadership actively acknowledges and appreciates achievements, it communicates the organization's values and reinforces a culture that values both individual and team accomplishments. Leaders can organize recognition events, express gratitude in meetings, or provide personalized commendations to highlight outstanding contributions.

In addition to formal recognition, creating rituals for celebrating successes as part of everyday work routines is equally important. This could include a brief acknowledgment during team meetings, a shout-out on collaboration platforms, or the ringing of a success bell in the office. These simple gestures contribute to a positive and celebratory atmosphere that becomes ingrained in the organizational culture. Furthermore, celebrating successes contributes to a positive narrative within the organization.

When employees see that their hard work leads to tangible outcomes and is met with appreciation, it creates a sense of pride in their work and their affiliation with the organization. This positive narrative not only attracts and retains talent but also contributes to a positive external reputation in the industry and the market. A real-world example of celebrating successes is found in a sales team that celebrated reaching a quarterly revenue goal. The leadership organized a team-wide recognition event, expressing gratitude for the collective effort and dedication. This celebration not only boosted team morale but also motivated individuals to continue their high-performance efforts in subsequent quarters.

In conclusion, celebrating successes, regardless of their size, is a foundational practice for cultivating a positive workplace culture. It enhances employee morale, strengthens team dynamics, and contributes to a narrative of achievement within the organization. By actively acknowledging and appreciating successes, leaders foster a culture that values continuous improvement, collaboration, and the collective pursuit of excellence. This intentional celebration of successes becomes a driving force for sustained employee engagement and overall organizational success.

Practical exercises for Reflection and Gratitude

Weekly Reflection Journal: Provide employees with a weekly reflection journal to record their professional achievements, challenges overcome, and moments of gratitude. This exercise encourages regular self-assessment and a mindset of appreciation.

Monthly Achievement Share-Out: Create a monthly forum where team members share their most significant professional achievements with the group. This fosters a culture of celebration and allows individuals to express gratitude for their accomplishments.

Gratitude Letter Writing: Encourage employees to write gratitude letters to colleagues, expressing appreciation for their contributions. This practice not only reinforces a positive work environment but also strengthens interpersonal relationships.

Reflection Circle During Team Meetings: Dedicate a few minutes in regular team meetings for a quick reflection circle. Each team member can share a recent success or express gratitude for the support they've received. This simple exercise builds camaraderie and positive energy within the team.

Daily Gratitude Log: Implement a daily gratitude log where employees note down three things they are thankful for in the workplace. This exercise prompts individuals to focus on positive aspects and fosters a mindset of gratitude.

Success Story Interviews: Conduct short interviews with team members who have achieved significant milestones. Share these success stories within the organization, allowing individuals to reflect on and appreciate the diverse accomplishments of their colleagues.

Team Building Retreat Reflections: After team-building retreats or workshops, provide structured reflection prompts. Encourage team members to reflect on what they learned, achievements during the event, and express gratitude for the opportunity to connect with colleagues.

Gratitude Wall: Establish a physical or virtual gratitude wall where team members can post notes of appreciation for their peers. This ongoing visual display reinforces a culture of gratitude and celebration within the workplace.

Success Story Webinars: Organize periodic webinars where team members present their success stories. This exercise provides a platform for individuals to reflect on their journeys, share insights, and express gratitude for the support they've received.

Year-End Gratitude and Reflection Ceremony: Host an annual ceremony where the organization collectively reflects on the year's achievements and expresses gratitude for the collaborative efforts. Recognize individual and team accomplishments, reinforcing a positive organizational culture.

These practical exercises and prompts for business reflection and gratitude are designed to be easily integrated into the workplace routine. By encouraging regular reflection and expressions of gratitude, organizations can foster a positive, appreciative culture that contributes to employee well-being, engagement, and overall team success.

NOVEMBER: WEALTH AND ABUNDANCE

Redefining Success and Wealth

In the evolving landscape of business, the redefinition of success and wealth is exemplified by the transformation of a multinational corporation. Traditionally focused solely on financial gains, the company underwent a strategic shift that reflected a broader understanding of success—one that prioritized purpose, sustainability, and social impact. The company, a global player in the consumer goods industry, recognized the changing expectations of consumers and stakeholders. Instead of solely emphasizing quarterly profits, leadership began to integrate sustainability goals into their corporate strategy. This shift was motivated not only by ethical considerations but also by a growing awareness that societal impact was becoming a significant factor in brand loyalty and market competitiveness. The company set ambitious targets to reduce its carbon footprint, implement eco-friendly packaging, and ensure responsible sourcing of raw materials. These initiatives not only aligned with global sustainability goals but also resonated with environmentally conscious consumers. As a result, the company witnessed an increase in market share and brand reputation.

Beyond environmental sustainability, the corporation embraced a people-centric approach to redefine success. Recognizing the importance of a healthy work environment and work-life balance, the company invested in employee wellness programs and flexible work arrangements. This focus on employee well-being not only improved overall morale but also positively impacted productivity and retention rates. Social impact became a key metric in the redefined notion of success for this corporation. The company actively engaged in community development projects, supporting local initiatives and addressing societal challenges. By channeling resources into education, healthcare, and infrastructure programs, the corporation demonstrated a commitment to being a responsible corporate citizen. The financial success of the company did not wane; in fact, it flourished. The strategic shift towards a more holistic definition of success contributed to increased customer loyalty, enhanced brand value, and improved investor confidence. The corporation's story serves as a factual illustration of how redefining success and wealth in a business context, with a focus on purpose and social responsibility, can lead to both financial prosperity and a positive impact on a broader scale.

This real-world example underscores the growing recognition within the business community that success extends beyond profit margins. By integrating values of sustainability, employee well-being, and social impact into their core strategies, companies are not only adapting to changing market dynamics but are also shaping a more responsible and purpose-driven business landscape.

Balancing Material Goals with Stoic Values

Balancing material goals with Stoic values in the business realm involves navigating the delicate intersection of ambition and ethical principles. Stoicism, with its emphasis on virtue, wisdom, and acceptance of what is beyond one's control, provides a philosophical framework for individuals and organizations seeking a harmonious integration of material success and ethical conduct. Stoicism encourages individuals to pursue goals with a focus on personal excellence rather than an obsessive attachment to external outcomes. In a business context, this translates to setting material goals such as revenue targets or market expansion, but with an understanding that these goals are pursued virtuously and in alignment with ethical principles. It involves cultivating a mindset where success is measured not only by financial gains but also by the ethical means through which those gains are achieved.

An illustrative example of balancing material goals with Stoic values can be found in the story of a tech startup. The company, driven by a desire for rapid growth, faced a dilemma when pressured to compromise on user data privacy to fuel its expansion. The leadership, influenced by Stoic principles, made a conscious decision to prioritize ethical conduct over immediate financial gains. Rather than succumbing to the temptation of exploiting user data for short-term profits, the company implemented robust privacy measures, transparently communicated their commitment to users, and invested in developing ethical data practices. This decision aligned with Stoic values of integrity and wisdom, emphasizing the importance of virtuous actions even in the face of external pressures. Balancing material goals with Stoic values also involves cultivating resilience in the face of setbacks and recognizing the limits of control. In business, unforeseen challenges are inevitable, and Stoicism encourages individuals to view these challenges as opportunities for growth rather than insurmountable obstacles. This perspective allows for a more measured and reasoned response to adversity, preventing the pursuit of material goals from becoming a source of undue stress. Stoicism further encourages individuals to differentiate between what is within their control and what is not. While material goals, such as achieving revenue targets, are set within one's control, external factors like market fluctuations are not. Acknowledging this distinction allows for a more measured approach to goal-setting, fostering a mindset that values the journey toward success as much as the destination.

In conclusion, balancing material goals with Stoic values in business involves embracing a philosophical approach that prioritizes virtue, ethical conduct, and resilience. It requires setting and pursuing material goals with a mindful awareness of the means employed and a recognition of the inherent uncertainties in the business landscape. By integrating Stoic principles into the pursuit of material success, individuals and organizations can foster a more meaningful, ethical, and resilient path to achieving their goals

Generosity and Philanthropy in Business

Generosity and philanthropy in business represent a transformative force that extends beyond profit margins, embodying a commitment to social responsibility and positive impact. In the modern corporate landscape, the integration of generosity and philanthropy is not only seen as a moral imperative but also as a strategic investment in building a sustainable and socially conscious brand. Generosity in business goes beyond financial contributions; it encompasses a culture of giving that permeates all levels of the organization. This culture is reflected in acts of kindness, support for employees facing challenges, and a genuine commitment to improving the well-being of both the internal workforce and external communities. Philanthropy, as a strategic extension of generosity, involves deliberate efforts to contribute to societal welfare. It goes beyond spontaneous acts of kindness, involving systematic initiatives to address social issues, support charitable causes, and contribute to the overall betterment of communities. Businesses engaging in philanthropy recognize their role as corporate citizens with the power to make a positive impact beyond their immediate operations.

An exemplary illustration of generosity and philanthropy in business can be found in a global tech company that allocates a percentage of its annual profits to various charitable causes. Beyond financial contributions, the company encourages employees to volunteer their time and skills to community initiatives. This dual approach not only supports external causes but also fosters a sense of purpose and fulfillment among employees, contributing to a positive workplace culture. In addition to fostering goodwill, generosity and philanthropy are becoming integral components of brand identity. Consumers increasingly value businesses that demonstrate a commitment to social and environmental responsibility. Companies that actively engage in philanthropy not only contribute to meaningful causes but also enhance their brand reputation, attracting socially conscious consumers and creating long-term brand loyalty. Generosity and philanthropy are also powerful tools for talent attraction and retention. The younger workforce, in particular, is drawn to organizations that align with their values and actively contribute to societal well-being. Companies that prioritize philanthropy as part of their organizational ethos are more likely to attract top-tier talent and retain employees who find purpose in their work beyond financial compensation.

The strategic integration of generosity and philanthropy into business practices underscores a shift toward a more compassionate and responsible capitalism. Beyond simply meeting legal and ethical standards, businesses are recognizing their potential to be agents of positive change. By actively participating in philanthropy and embodying a culture of generosity, organizations contribute not only to the well-being of communities but also to their own sustained success in an increasingly socially conscious marketplace.

Practical exercises for Wealth and Abundance

Gratitude Journal for Business Success: Start a gratitude journal specifically focused on business achievements. Regularly write down three things related to your business for which you are grateful. This practice fosters a mindset of abundance and appreciates the positive aspects of your professional journey.

Abundance Affirmations: Develop a set of positive affirmations related to wealth and abundance in your business. Repeat these affirmations daily to reinforce a positive mindset and attract abundance into your professional life.

Prosperity Visualization Exercise: Set aside time each week for a guided visualization session focused on the prosperity and growth of your business. Envision successful outcomes, increased revenue, and a flourishing work environment.

Share Your Success Story: Write a detailed account of your business successes, milestones, and achievements. Share this story with your team, clients, or stakeholders to celebrate accomplishments and reinforce a collective sense of abundance.

Financial Goal Setting and Tracking: Clearly define financial goals for your business and create a tracking system to monitor progress. Regularly review and update these goals to maintain a focus on abundance and financial success.

Collaborative Abundance Mindset Workshop: Host a workshop with your team to discuss and cultivate an abundance mindset. Encourage open dialogue about opportunities, shared successes, and collaborative approaches to achieving abundance in the business.

Generosity Challenge: Initiate a generosity challenge within your organization. Encourage team members to engage in acts of kindness, support one another, or contribute to a shared cause. This practice fosters a culture of abundance and giving.

Financial Abundance Meditation: Incorporate a brief financial abundance meditation into your daily routine. Focus on feelings of prosperity, envisioning the positive impact of financial success on your business and personal life.

Abundance Board: Create a visual representation of abundance by developing an abundance board. Include images, quotes, and symbols that represent the wealth and success you envision for your business. Display this board in your workspace for daily inspiration.

Abundance Reflection Sessions: Schedule regular reflection sessions where you and your team discuss instances of abundance and success in the business. Reflecting on positive outcomes reinforces a mindset of abundance and encourages a proactive approach to seeking and creating wealth.

These practical exercises and prompts for business wealth and abundance are designed to shift the focus toward positive and prosperous thinking. By incorporating these practices into your routine and fostering a culture of abundance within your organization, you contribute to a mindset that attracts and sustains financial success in your business endeavors.

DECEMBER: LEGACY AND IMPACT

Building a Lasting Legacy

Building a lasting legacy in business goes beyond immediate success and financial achievements; it involves creating a sustained impact that extends beyond the individual or company. Whether as an entrepreneur, executive, or business leader, the pursuit of a lasting legacy requires a deliberate and thoughtful approach that encompasses both personal and professional dimensions. One crucial aspect of building a lasting legacy is aligning personal values with business practices. This integration ensures that the legacy reflects not only financial success but also a commitment to ethical conduct, social responsibility, and positive contributions to society. By adhering to a set of core values, leaders can create a legacy that transcends the business realm, resonating with a broader audience.

A real-world example of building a lasting legacy is evident in the story of a family-owned manufacturing business. Over generations, the leadership of the company prioritized sustainability, innovation, and community engagement. Instead of solely focusing on short-term profits, they invested in eco-friendly practices, cutting-edge technology, and initiatives that benefited the local community. The commitment to these values not only positioned the business as an industry leader but also contributed to a positive legacy. The company's name became synonymous with responsible business practices,

125

environmental stewardship, and community support. This enduring legacy not only attracted loyal customers but also positioned the business as a model for sustainable and socially conscious entrepreneurship.

Another key element in building a lasting legacy is mentorship and knowledge sharing. Leaders who actively mentor and develop the next generation of professionals contribute to a legacy that extends beyond their own tenure. By sharing experiences, insights, and skills, they create a ripple effect that impacts the industry and fosters a culture of continuous learning and improvement. Strategic philanthropy is also integral to building a lasting legacy. Companies and individuals that engage in philanthropic endeavors aligned with their values contribute to positive societal change. Establishing foundations, supporting educational initiatives, or addressing pressing social issues through targeted philanthropy ensures that the legacy extends to making a meaningful impact on the world. Furthermore, effective communication plays a vital role in building a lasting legacy. Leaders who transparently communicate their vision, values, and long-term goals inspire trust and loyalty. A legacy is not only about the impact during one's active career but also about how it is communicated and remembered by those who follow.

In conclusion, building a lasting legacy in business is a multifaceted endeavor that requires a combination of strategic thinking, ethical leadership, and a commitment to positive impact. By aligning personal values with business practices, fostering mentorship, engaging in strategic philanthropy, and communicating transparently, leaders can create a legacy that transcends the immediate business landscape, leaving a lasting and positive imprint on the industry and society as a whole.

Measuring Success beyond Profit

Measuring success beyond profit is a paradigm shift that acknowledges the broader impact businesses can have on society, the environment, and the well-being of individuals. While financial success remains a crucial metric, there is a growing recognition that a comprehensive assessment of success encompasses a range of factors that contribute to the greater good. This perspective aligns with the principles of conscious capitalism and sustainable business practices. One essential dimension of measuring success beyond profit involves evaluating the social impact of a business. Companies that actively engage in corporate social responsibility (CSR) initiatives, community development projects, and philanthropy contribute positively to societal well-being. Metrics such as the number of lives impacted, community partnerships established, and environmental sustainability efforts undertaken become integral components of assessing success.

An exemplary illustration of measuring success beyond profit is found in the story of a tech company that not only achieved financial success but also prioritized social impact. The company implemented initiatives to bridge the digital divide, providing access to technology and education in underserved communities. By measuring success through the number of students impacted and improvements in educational outcomes, the company demonstrated a commitment to a broader and more inclusive definition of success. Environmental sustainability is another critical factor in assessing success beyond profit. Businesses that adopt eco-friendly practices, reduce their carbon footprint, and prioritize sustainable sourcing contribute to a healthier planet. Metrics such as reduced waste, increased use of renewable energy, and adherence to environmentally friendly production processes become key indicators of success in this context. Employee well-being and workplace culture are significant aspects of measuring success beyond profit. Companies that prioritize the health, happiness, and professional development of their employees create a positive work environment. Metrics such as employee satisfaction, retention rates, and opportunities for professional growth provide insights into the holistic success of a business. Moreover, customer satisfaction and brand reputation play a pivotal role in this expanded definition of success. Businesses that prioritize ethical practices, transparency, and customer-centric approaches cultivate loyalty and positive brand perception. Metrics related to customer feedback, brand recognition, and ethical ratings contribute to a comprehensive assessment of success.

In conclusion, measuring success beyond profit reflects a contemporary understanding of the multifaceted impact businesses can have on various stakeholders. Beyond financial metrics, success is evaluated through social impact, environmental sustainability, employee well-being, and ethical business practices. This holistic approach aligns with evolving societal expectations and positions businesses as contributors to positive change in the world, fostering a sustainable and conscious business landscape.

Leaving a Positive Impact on the World

Leaving a positive impact on the world through business involves a purpose-driven approach that extends beyond profit margins to address societal challenges, environmental concerns, and the well-being of communities. This commitment to creating a positive legacy aligns with the principles of social responsibility and conscious capitalism, recognizing that businesses have a unique role in contributing to the greater good.

One fundamental aspect of leaving a positive impact is embracing corporate social responsibility (CSR) as a core business practice. Companies that integrate CSR initiatives into their operations actively contribute to social causes, community development, and sustainable practices. By allocating resources to philanthropy, supporting local initiatives, and promoting ethical conduct, businesses become agents of positive change in the communities they serve. An illustrative example of leaving a positive impact is evident in the story of a global fashion brand that implemented fair trade and sustainability practices. The company committed to ethically sourcing materials, ensuring fair wages for workers, and minimizing environmental impact. By leaving a smaller ecological footprint and positively influencing supply chain practices, the company demonstrated how businesses can contribute to a more sustainable and socially responsible industry. Environmental stewardship is a crucial dimension of leaving a positive impact on the world. Businesses that prioritize eco-friendly practices, energy efficiency, and carbon neutrality actively contribute to the global effort to address climate change. Initiatives such as reducing single-use plastics, investing in renewable energy sources, and implementing green manufacturing processes demonstrate a commitment to leaving a positive environmental legacy.

In addition to environmental considerations, businesses can positively impact the world by prioritizing diversity, equity, and inclusion (DEI) within their organizations. Creating a workplace culture that values diversity and actively promotes inclusivity contributes to societal progress. Companies that prioritize DEI not only foster a positive internal environment but also set an example for industry peers and contribute to dismantling systemic inequalities. Another essential aspect of leaving a positive impact is engaging in partnerships and collaborations that address social issues. By forming alliances with non-profit organizations, governmental bodies, and other businesses, companies can amplify their impact on pressing societal challenges. This collaborative approach enables businesses to leverage their resources and expertise for the greater good. Measuring success in terms of the positive impact on the world involves evaluating key performance indicators beyond financial metrics. Metrics such as social impact assessments, carbon footprint reduction, employee satisfaction, and community outreach initiatives become integral components of assessing the holistic success of a business.

In conclusion, leaving a positive impact on the world through business requires a holistic and intentional approach. By embracing corporate social responsibility, prioritizing environmental sustainability, fostering diversity and inclusion, and engaging in collaborative efforts, businesses can actively contribute to positive societal change. This commitment not only aligns with evolving societal expectations but also positions businesses as key contributors to creating a more equitable, sustainable, and compassionate world.

Practical exercises for Legacy and Impact

Legacy Statement Crafting: Engage in a reflective exercise to articulate your personal and business legacy. Write a statement that encapsulates the impact you aspire to leave on your industry, community, and the world.

Stakeholder Impact Mapping: Identify key stakeholders, including employees, customers, communities, and the environment. Map out the positive impact your business can have on each group and develop strategies to enhance these contributions.

Historical Review Workshop: Conduct a workshop where employees explore the history and milestones of the business. Encourage discussions on the positive contributions the company has made and how these contributions have shaped its legacy.

Sustainability Audit: Evaluate your business practices through a sustainability lens. Assess energy consumption, waste management, and supply chain ethics. Develop a plan to enhance sustainability practices, leaving a positive environmental legacy.

Legacy Vision Board: Create a visual representation of your business legacy through a vision board. Include images, quotes, and symbols that align with the impact you want to leave. Display the board in a prominent place to inspire and remind stakeholders of the legacy vision.

Employee Impact Stories: Encourage employees to share personal stories about how the company's initiatives or values have positively impacted their lives. Compile these stories into a collection that highlights the human side of the business legacy.

Community Engagement Challenge: Challenge your team to identify and execute community engagement initiatives. This could involve volunteering, supporting local causes, or collaborating with community organizations. Measure and celebrate the impact created.

Ethical Decision-Making Workshops: Conduct workshops on ethical decision-making within the company. Equip employees with the tools to make principled choices, reinforcing a culture of integrity that contributes to the long-term positive legacy of the business.

Leadership Succession Planning: Develop a leadership succession plan that emphasizes continuity of the business legacy. Identify potential leaders who embody the values and vision essential for sustaining and building upon the positive impact of the company.

Impact Metrics Dashboard: Create a comprehensive metrics dashboard that tracks the impact of the business on various aspects, including social, environmental, and employee well-being. Regularly review and update these metrics to ensure alignment with the desired legacy and impact.

These practical exercises and prompts for business legacy and impact are designed to be actionable and foster a culture of intentionality in creating positive and lasting contributions. By engaging in these exercises, businesses can actively shape their legacy and leave a meaningful impact on stakeholders and the broader community.

CONCLUSION

In conclusion, the journey toward creating a meaningful and lasting legacy in business involves a deliberate and conscious effort to go beyond traditional measures of success. While financial prosperity is undoubtedly important, the impact a business leaves on its stakeholders, community, and the world at large is increasingly recognized as a key indicator of true success. Throughout this exploration of various dimensions, from embracing stoic principles to measuring success beyond profit and leaving a positive impact on the world, a common thread emerges—the need for businesses to operate with a sense of purpose and responsibility. Building a legacy that extends beyond the individual or the bottom line requires a holistic approach that considers the ethical, social, and environmental implications of business decisions. By adopting stoic principles, entrepreneurs and business leaders can cultivate resilience, ethical decision-making, and a focus on what is within their control. This philosophical framework not only enhances personal well-being but also contributes to the development of a resilient and principled business culture. Measuring success beyond profit involves a shift in perspective, acknowledging the interconnectedness of business with broader societal and environmental contexts. It requires businesses to actively engage in corporate social responsibility, prioritize environmental sustainability, and create workplaces that foster diversity and inclusion.

Leaving a positive impact on the world through business requires a commitment to ethical practices, sustainability, and community engagement. Real-world examples illustrate how businesses can align their values with their operations to contribute positively to society while maintaining financial success. As businesses strive to build a legacy and impact that outlasts their immediate operations, practical exercises play a crucial role. Crafting a legacy statement, mapping stakeholder impact, and engaging in sustainability audits are just a few examples of tangible actions that can guide businesses toward their desired legacy. In the pursuit of a lasting legacy, businesses have the power to shape not only their industry landscape but also the broader societal narrative. By actively considering the ethical implications of their actions, fostering a culture of sustainability and responsibility, and engaging in purpose-driven initiatives, businesses can contribute to a more positive and compassionate world.

In essence, the conclusion drawn is that the journey toward building a lasting legacy in business is an ongoing process of self-reflection, conscious decision-making, and a commitment to values that extend beyond immediate financial gains. As businesses embark on this journey, they have the opportunity to redefine success, leave a positive impact, and contribute to a legacy that resonates with principles of purpose, resilience, and responsible capitalism.

Recap of Key Lessons

As we reflect on the exploration of daily stoic meditations for entrepreneurs and the broader themes of building a lasting legacy, several key lessons emerge that encapsulate the essence of this journey. These lessons serve as guiding principles for entrepreneurs and business leaders seeking to navigate the intersection of stoicism, ethical business practices, and a commitment to positive impact.

Firstly, the incorporation of stoic principles into the daily lives of entrepreneurs offers valuable insights into resilience, adaptability, and the power of perspective. The lessons drawn from Stoicism encourage individuals to focus on what is within their control, accept the inevitability of challenges, and cultivate an unwavering commitment to virtue in both personal and professional endeavors. The exploration of measuring success beyond profit underscores the importance of redefining traditional metrics of success. Businesses are increasingly recognizing that success extends beyond financial gains to encompass social impact, environmental sustainability, and employee well-being. The recalibration of success metrics aligns with evolving societal expectations and positions businesses as contributors to positive change. Leaving a positive impact on the world through business emerges as a central theme, emphasizing the interconnectedness of business decisions with broader societal and environmental contexts. The lessons learned highlight the significance of corporate social responsibility, sustainable practices, and ethical decision-making in shaping a positive legacy that extends beyond individual achievements. Practical exercises and prompts for business legacy and impact provide actionable steps for translating these lessons into tangible outcomes. Crafting a legacy statement, engaging in sustainability audits, and fostering a culture of diversity and inclusion are among the exercises designed to guide businesses toward their desired legacy. A recurring theme throughout this exploration is the importance of purpose-driven business practices. Whether through stoic principles, ethical decision-making, or community engagement, the alignment of business operations with a higher purpose is foundational to building a meaningful and lasting legacy.

In summary, the key lessons learned from this journey underscore the importance of cultivating resilience, redefining success metrics, leaving a positive impact on the world, and engaging in purpose-driven initiatives. As entrepreneurs and business leaders integrate these lessons into their daily practices, they have the opportunity to shape not only the trajectory of their businesses but also to contribute positively to the broader narrative of responsible and conscious capitalism. The journey toward building a lasting legacy is an ongoing process of reflection, adaptation, and a commitment to values that transcend immediate gains, fostering a business culture that resonates with principles of virtue, impact, and purpose.

The Continuous Practice of Stoic Entrepreneurship

The continuous practice of Stoic entrepreneurship represents an ongoing commitment to embodying stoic principles in the ever-evolving landscape of business. As entrepreneurs navigate the challenges, uncertainties, and opportunities inherent in their endeavors, the application of stoic philosophy serves as a steadfast guide for ethical decision-making, resilience, and personal growth. Stoicism, with its roots in ancient philosophy, remains profoundly relevant in the context of modern entrepreneurship. One key lesson derived from Stoicism is the emphasis on distinguishing between what is within one's control and what is not. Entrepreneurs, faced with myriad external factors, find solace and empowerment in focusing their efforts on aspects they can influence, fostering a sense of agency in the face of uncertainty.

The continuous practice of Stoic entrepreneurship also emphasizes the cultivation of resilience. Stoicism teaches entrepreneurs to view challenges as opportunities for growth and learning rather than insurmountable obstacles. By embracing setbacks with a stoic mindset, entrepreneurs develop the mental fortitude needed to persevere in the dynamic and often unpredictable business environment. Furthermore, the concept of negative visualization, a stoic exercise involving contemplating potential challenges and setbacks, prepares entrepreneurs for adversity. This proactive approach enables them to develop contingency plans, mitigate risks, and navigate uncertainties with a sense of preparedness and equanimity. The stoic principle of living in accordance with nature translates into a call for ethical business practices. Continuous self-examination and adherence to virtuous principles guide entrepreneurs in making decisions that align with their values and contribute positively to the well-being of stakeholders and the broader community. In the realm of Stoic entrepreneurship, the practice of mindfulness plays a pivotal role. Entrepreneurs are encouraged to be present, fully engaged in the tasks at hand, and mindful of the impact of their decisions. This heightened awareness fosters a more intentional approach to entrepreneurship, reducing the likelihood of impulsive actions driven by external pressures. The application of Stoicism in entrepreneurship is not a one-time endeavor but a continuous journey of self-discovery and improvement. Regular self-reflection, the incorporation of stoic exercises into daily routines, and an unwavering commitment to virtuous conduct contribute to the cultivation of a stoic mindset that becomes ingrained in the entrepreneur's approach to business.

In conclusion, the continuous practice of Stoic entrepreneurship offers a timeless and invaluable framework for entrepreneurs seeking not only financial success but also personal fulfillment, ethical leadership, and a positive impact on the world. As entrepreneurs embrace the stoic principles of resilience, mindfulness, and ethical decision-making, they embark on a transformative journey that transcends immediate challenges, contributing to the development of a purpose-driven and enduring legacy in the realm of business.

www.ingramcontent.com/pod-product-compliance
Lightning Source LLC
Chambersburg PA
CBHW071046290526
45795CB00004B/1354